"*How to Help Others without l*... the reader's attention while p... exercises for those of us in 'helping' professions. Whether you need a quick boost to better deal with on-the-job stress or a reminder of what you do well, this book will make you reassess the many positive contributions you are making to those around you. An invaluable addition to the bookshelf."

MATTHEW BRANDON, BSW, LLB
Family Law Lawyer and former Social Worker

"An excellent resource for those in the helping professions—kernels of wisdom to assist helpers navigate the murky issues facing those in their care. The appendices contain invaluable resources and activities to maintain a sense of balance and integrity so important to one's quality of life. Thank you for taking the time out of your busy life to write a 'how-to' manual designed to improve the lives of those in the helping professions!"

SUSAN JOHNSON, BA, PDP and **M.ED**
Teacher-in-Charge at the Cloverdale Learning Centre
(alternate setting for at-risk youth)

"In *How To Help Others without Losing Yourself,* Debbie Holmes tackles, head on, the all too common issues of emotional fatigue and burnout among helping professionals. Whether you are new to the helping field or a seasoned professional, you are sure to find helpful self-care tips and strategies in this book."

MARK FLYNN, B.ED., MSW, RCC, RSW
Clinical Counsellor

How to Help Others

WITHOUT LOSING YOURSELF

DEBBIE HOLMES

Library and Archives Canada Cataloguing in Publication

Holmes, Debbie, 1971–, author
        How to help others without losing yourself / Debbie Holmes.

Issued in print and electronic formats.
ISBN 978-0-9936060-0-7 (pbk.).—ISBN 978-0-9936060-1-4 (ebook)

        1. Human services personnel—Psychology. 2. Burn out (Psychology)—Prevention. I. Title.

HV41.H64 2014   361.3023   C2013-908232-8
                                                             C2013-908285-9

Front cover photograph by Harry Warkentin
Author photograph by Paul Keeris
Editing by Melanie Berezan
Book design by Fiona Raven

First Printing 2014
Printed in the USA

Published by
Powerful Paths Publishing

www.DebbieHolmes.ca

To all Helpers, this book is for you.

Please take the time to care for yourself as much as
you are taking care of others!

Acknowledgements

I cannot say enough about my first readers: the many people who read my book to make sure the content worked and the grammar and spelling was correct. Thanks to all of you for helping me create an amazing finished product.

Fiona Raven, thank you for your hard work and dedication. You've made my book cover and pages look so professional. You were so easy to work with and took the time to make sure everything was done well and was exactly what I wanted.

Thank you to Harry from Harry's Images for the cover photograph. I really appreciate your effort and dedication to the project. You are not only a phenomenal photographer but a great friend.

I cannot say enough about my editor and chief advisor for all her help throughout the writing—Melanie Berezan. She took the raw script and helped me transform it into a phenomenal end product. I could not have completed this project without her guidance and support.

To my working partner Mark—you have been an inspiration and I would not have been able to take the step to actually write this book if you had not been so supportive. You are a great counsellor and I only hope others will be inspired the way I have.

To my trainer Scott—you have taught me the tough-love lessons I needed to have confidence in myself and my abilities. You believed in me when I did not and taught me to move forward and break down my own barriers.

To my dearest friend Natalie—I cannot thank you enough for all the support you have given me through the years. When we met I never once thought we would end up the best of friends. You have helped me to heal my spirit and guide me forward to this moment for which I am truly grateful. Thank you.

I want to thank my in-laws; Gerry for teaching me how to find that rare book in a thrift store that could only enhance the research for this book, and Jill, for teaching me how to accept everyone with grace and elegance.

I want to thank my parents, who taught me about values and to continue to strive for my dreams—no matter what obstacles were put in my path—and good things will happen. I admire how you were able to raise five children and still always found the time to be there for our activities. We were always first!

To my brothers, sisters, and sisters in-law, thank you for the support and enthusiasm I got when you found out that I wrote a book. Your unique character and enjoyment for life have helped me in more ways than you will ever know.

I was lucky enough to know most of my grandparents for a long time. To Grandma Keller, who taught me how to do the simple things in life like growing vegetables and canning fruit; I miss you so much. To Grandma Maggie, who taught me how to slow down and crochet when I needed to sort out my thoughts; thank you. Sadly neither is able to fully see the end of my dream turn into a reality, but I know they would have bragged to all their friends if given the opportunity.

To my children, you are the reason I get up every day. Thank you for inspiring me and encouraging me to continue working on the book even though sometimes it interfered with your activities. I love you both so much.

To my soulmate Bob. You inspire me with your positive spirit and love. Without your support, I don't think my journey would have been as extensive as it has been. I am looking forward to the many tomorrows we are going to share.

Contents

List of Appendices

Introduction

Sometimes we don't know where life will take us, but I always knew my path. From the age of four, it was my dream to become a teacher. When friends came to my house to play I would make them play "school" with me—even though most of them hated to do so—and I was always the teacher. When I was in elementary school I would dream it was me at the front of the room teaching the students. When I was in high school all the vocational surveys I completed suggested I become a teacher. During that time I was able to work for our community Parks and Recreation department teaching courses to children, and one of my high school teachers (who later become my mentor in the teaching profession) gave me an opportunity to teach a lesson to his class in my senior year. These two tastes of teaching sealed the deal for me. I loved it! Being a teacher was my goal and I was determined to become a teacher, one way or another.

My dream of being a teacher was as important to me as getting married and having children. Over the years I have been able to realize each of my dreams but along the way I came up against some pretty big obstacles.

When I started university I struggled but I had no clue why I wasn't doing as well academically as I had in high school. I was placed on academic probation and I will never forget how dejected I felt. I was filled with self-doubt. I began to believe I would never become a teacher—especially if I could not even make it through my first-year history courses. And while my family supported my dream to become a teacher, because they helped me out with my tuition, I felt pressure to do well. I feared that on the surface it appeared to them as though I was slacking off.

I became demoralized by the ongoing struggle and after a long period of frustration I was ready to quit school. It didn't help that I had two professors who told me I might as well quit because I was never going to graduate. Hearing their words was so devastating for me. I was desperate to become a teacher and I was terrified of not attaining my dream. I think back now to how naïve I was then and how I did not defend myself. I believed that because they were university professors they knew more than me. I see now that I gave them all the power they were demanding (a lesson I've learned since: we must teach people how we want to be treated—see Chapter 1, Respecting Yourself and Others). But at that time I did not know any better.

But my circumstance did not come about from lack of trying: I was a slow reader and it always took me so long to understand what I read. Most of the time we had to read novels or multiple chapters per course each week and as a slow reader, I was drowning in my homework.

However, a few key people in my life encouraged me to continue my journey and somehow, I persevered.

I eventually reached fourth year university. Slowly I'd worked my way off academic probation and was able to apply for entry into the teaching program. But then I had difficulties getting into the program; my grades were not high enough. I had been working with children leading recreational courses and teaching preschool but despite my practical experience, academically, my best did not seem good enough. In essence I had to learn to play the game of life to survive this storm. I had to play by their rules. I needed to update my schooling and take the courses that the administrators of the teaching program favoured. Recreational work was not the only experience they were looking for; I also needed to volunteer in an actual classroom with a trained professional. Once I realized what they were specifically looking for, I started working on improving my application.

This was not a fast process. I applied for and was denied entry into the program three times. Finally, on the fourth attempt I was accepted. I had finally figured out what experience they wanted me to focus on and I had gone out and done the work that was necessary for a solid application.

Once I was finally accepted I couldn't believe it. It felt surreal after all the previous attempts and rejections. When it finally sunk in that I was really, truly on the path to becoming a teacher I was so proud of myself I felt nothing else was ever going to stand in my way again. I had accomplished what I needed so that my dream would come true. I was finally where I needed to be. Now that I was in the teaching program everything else would fall into place. Or so I thought.

After obtaining my teaching certificate, it was time for me to get a job. Little did I know that this would be another challenge. My practicum teacher wrote a reference letter for me that outlined all the areas I needed to work on without accentuating my strengths. This was a problem; it was supposed to be a reference letter, not an evaluation. I don't believe I am perfect and there were definitely areas I could improve on, but there were also many things I could do well. Unfortunately, none of my strengths were mentioned. This letter did not make me look employable at all.

I did not even find this out until—after I failed to secure a single job interview—I asked to obtain a copy of the sealed reference letter that she had sent in on my behalf. Once again I needed to be proactive and find a way to navigate this challenge. I am not one to sit on the sidelines and wait for something to happen—I am the type of person who gives myself a short period of mourning time and then I pick myself up and figure out how I am going to solve the problem.

With some help from the network of people I knew in the education system, I was finally able to secure a job interview and was hired right away as a substitute teacher. My childhood dream was finally realized: I was a teacher with a paying job.

When I reflect back now on that part of my journey, I think the main lesson I learned is that asking for help did not mean I was "weak" (see Chapter 2, Asking for Help and Creating Support). It was okay to ask for help from those who were in a position to help me. It is what we do with the help that is offered that matters most. We can use help wisely or we can squander it, but there is always an opportunity to create in ourselves the person we want to be. And now, at this point in my career, I am in a position to help other people or colleagues that need support. This is my way of paying it forward.

Another lesson I learned is that while it is natural to feel self-pity when things don't work out, at some point we need to figure out what is wrong and address the issue (see Chapter 6, Challenges Helpers Face). It is more beneficial to push ahead instead of focusing on the past and *poor me*. Other people cannot stop us from fulfilling our dreams in life; only we can. We create who we want to be. If I had not taken the time to figure this out I never would have embraced new challenges and exciting opportunities or grown as I have.

My parents always told my siblings and I that we had to work hard and strive for what we wanted. If I hadn't learned that lesson from my family I don't believe I would have had the successes in my life that I do today. And it is only because I learned to persevere and deal with issues that I have become the strong, confident woman that I am.

I am grateful for all the opportunities I was given, even when they were disguised as obstacles. When I was young I thought I wanted to teach at the elementary school level, preferably grade six. I did not even consider teaching at the high school level. I guess I did not believe I would be able to connect with teenagers because I did not do well socially in high school myself (another example of where I let self-doubt creep in—see Chapter 7, Knocking out Negativity, Fear and Self-Doubt). In what ultimately turned out to be a stroke of luck for me, there were no jobs open at the elementary school level so I accepted my first post in a high school. And when I started teaching I was very surprised how much I really enjoyed working with teenagers. In fact, I've never looked back.

In Chapter 1, I discuss my belief that my success in teaching teen-agers has come from the fact that I respect them for who they are at that moment in time, without judgment. In turn, they respect me as a teacher. As adults we want to be respected. Youth are no different; they feel the same way. This reminds me of the old adage, "Don't judge a book by its cover." If we don't want people to judge us, then we need to do the same with our clients (or the people we are working with).

I have never shied away from problems—although sometimes I will not have the energy to deal with them right in the moment. I need to continually remind myself that this is okay. There are so many problems that come up for us and our clients in a day; it can be overwhelming. Trying to solve them all at the same time can be difficult. Sometimes we need to limit the issues we focus on at once so we can take the appropriate amount of time to be successful, and address remaining issues at another time.

I learned valuable lessons through my youth and young adult life in dealing with struggles with my weight and other social issues. Those experiences have given me empathy for what my clients have to struggle through today. For example, I was a year younger in school because of where my birthday fell in the calendar year. As a result, sometimes I would feel overwhelmed and not emotionally or socially prepared for the changes that were coming my way. I felt like I was being pushed into things that I did not want to do or wasn't ready for. In the end, I caught up emotionally and socially, but I spent a lot of my time through my teen years feeling awkward and like I did not belong.

One key to working as a Helper is the ability to feel empathy for our clients without taking on (or taking home) their problems (see Chapter 2, Asking for Help and Creating Support). It can be easy to say, hard to do! As Helpers, we want to help but we tend to burn ourselves out in the process. And many times, we just keep going back for more. It is almost like being addicted to work (isn't it funny that most people frown upon addictions, except when it comes to being addicted to work?). Many Helpers are addicted to work as well as the consequent feeling of accomplishment that working in a helping profession can create. Another name for this is "workaholism". There has been more and more research on workaholism and self-help groups have been formed in many communities to help address this issue.

Anne Schaef and Diane Fassel wrote a compelling book, *The Addictive Organization,* about this subject. They talk about how people can give so much of themselves that they become a co-dependent to the organization they work for. A co-dependent is a person who depends on other people to make themself feel better. This behavior is an external avenue one may pursue in order to feel valued. That is, instead of generating value intrinsically, from within themselves, they seek the feeling from an external source: validation from the person or people they are helping. Further, Schaef and Fassel reveal that many people who suffer from this type of addiction are professional Helpers:

> Co-dependents frequently spend much of their time tak-ing care of others. Many enter professions that allow them to continue caring for others: nursing, counseling, social work, the ministry, medicine, psychology. Those who work with co-dependents report that they have low self-esteem and will literally kill themselves to be liked by others.[1]

Another trap co-dependents fall into is not feeling worthy. In the case of Helpers this may result in the need to make themselves indebted to others. Helpers like to feel irreplaceable (again, seeking value and self-worth extrinsically), which often leads to workaholism. In Schaef and Fassel's words:

> Co-dependents are sufferers. They are selfless to the point of illness.... Co-dependents complain a lot, but when you offer to help, they refuse your help—not wanting to burden you and preferring, in their illusion of control and self-centeredness, to do it themselves. Co-dependents carry an identifiable constella-tion of diseases. They tend toward ulcers, high blood pressure, colitis, back pain, and certain types of cancer. It is believed that, like the disease of addiction, co-dependence is a fatal disease.[2]

This may read as an extreme example, but it is a trap that I myself have fallen into, and I am hoping to help prevent others from making the same mistakes.

As Helpers we spend all this time taking care of people and sometimes it seems there is no one left to take care of us. The trap we can fall into is forgetting the people around us, and, even worse, not letting them feel needed or letting them help us out. We need others to be supportive of us. We need to balance helping with being helped. We need to remember we should not strive to be irreplaceable. Why not? Here's why: when I gave everything to others it left nothing for me or my family. Over time, I developed serious health problems. In short, my body wasn't shy to tell me what my mind wouldn't admit. Until I regained balance in my life, my health did not improve. This is one of the reasons I have written this book: to help others before they make the same mistake.

There are other valuable lessons I've learned. My immediate family all works in the private sector and, over the years, while sitting at the dinner table I have listened to many talks about what they have learned from the different ventures they have undertaken. I have been able to apply some of those lessons to my career as a helping professional, for example marrying my career as a teacher with the desire to reach others on a larger scale.

My siblings and I also share a strong drive to succeed, but we've learned that to be successful we need to work smarter, not just harder. Sometimes we have to go through numerous professional aches and pains to learn this lesson. Learning to slow down is very important as we all need to recharge, in body and in spirit. We need to ensure we have set up and maintained healthy boundaries so we don't bring our work home with us, which is a trap that as Helpers we tend to fall into (see Chapter 5, Developing Boundaries with Patience and Flexibility).

It is interesting to note that growing up my family was (and still is) big on sitting down and having dinner together. Even now, as adults, my siblings and I and our respective families are regularly invited to Sunday night dinners. My mom and dad have always believed it is important to communicate with each other and the tradition of family dinner continues to be the perfect opportunity to do so. We are better communicators because of the value we place on this tradition and it is a good reminder that we need to build values into our lives (see Chapter 4, Values).

Sometimes the best intentions go awry. A while ago, I was at a funeral for a friend who had fostered children for more than thirty years. She had made a positive impact on so many people. Her selflessness was inspiring to me and I wanted to do more with my life. Unfortunately, while my intentions were noble, this ended up being a big mistake because I ended up becoming too driven and gave too much of myself while pursing my goal.

At the time of this epiphany, my children were eight and five. I worked full time because we needed the double income to support the lifestyle we were living—and let's face it, kids at any age are expensive. Then I decided to start a non-profit organization to work with youth who had anger issues. Working and running a non-profit organization wasn't enough for me, so I decided to enroll as a full-time weekend student in a drug counselling program at university. The result? I had no time to do anything because all my free time was spent doing homework or studying. Everyone suffered—my family, my students and especially, my husband.

Luckily for me, it was around this time that I had the opportunity to see Anthony Robbins speak at the "Power Within" series.[3] It changed my life! Anthony Robbins is a fascinating and electrifying speaker and his presentation left a deep impression on me (not to mention the fact that Anthony Robbins was able to get 8,000 businesspeople hugging each other all at the same time). Distilled into one sentence, his message was that we create our own destinies and if there are things lacking in our lives then we need to address them. At the time, I thought I was doing just that. I knew what I wanted or needed to do and I was living the life I had always dreamed. Everything was perfect and I didn't have to worry about anything, I just needed to survive this crazy year and my life would improve immensely. Boy, was I further from the truth than I realized.

The next day I slipped and cracked my head open. I ended up with six stitches and a concussion. I was not allowed to do anything for a few days except lay in bed with ice on my head and face. I have never made a good sick person because being sick required me to slow down; now I was forced to rest and, consequently, I had a lot of time to reflect about my life. And I realized something shocking: I did not have it all "together", like I'd thought I did. I realized that while I was helping others professionally, I was losing myself and my family in the process.

Then the negative self-talk began—What in the world was I doing? If I couldn't even help myself how could I consider myself successful? All sorts of questions ran through my head. It was a difficult process to work through. Ultimately, however, I realized this was not a negative situation but an opportunity. It was time to reset my goals, to make sure I stayed true to my personal boundaries and to start changing my focus in life. Sometimes slowing down to get perspective can truly be a life changing experience.

When I was upright again, I made lists of ways I could help people and calculated how I could work with youth without devoting my whole self to my work. I went about making both short- and long-term goals (see Chapter 9, Knowing Yourself). A wise colleague once told me that if one has the skills to do so, one can help thousands of people by developing programs. This was a clarifying moment for me because I realized from his advice that by writing a book I could potentially help many people (or at the very least I'd help the twenty relatives that will buy the book from me because we were taught that family supports each other; there are some advantages to having a large family). Writing this book became one of my goals for my new, balanced life. I would work smarter, not harder.

I have also learned there are times when we need to "hibernate" to work on our inner-selves, and there are times when we need to work on our outer-selves. When you lose yourself to others, parts of you suffer too. At times I've felt that I was losing my identity, and when one aspect of my life was off balance, my health paid for it.

There are many examples of this in the teaching profession. We tend to take on big projects that can keep us very busy. One year, my colleague and I decided to take on four very large projects on top of teaching the students we already had. These four projects became like four additional jobs and they left us with no time for ourselves. I did not go to the gym as regularly as I should have and I tended to take work home with me daily. Time with my children started to suffer. We almost killed ourselves to run some pretty great projects for others. The next school year we both suffered from some major health issues. I was on the better end; my colleague had a life-threatening illness. What I learned from that year was that we were very good at getting money for other projects, but we did not think through the implementation. We gave so much more to other people without thinking of the consequences to ourselves. This was the wake-up call we needed to keep us continuing to do good work but to stay healthy while doing it. I truly believe the universe has a way of telling you to slow down. You just need to stop and listen once in a while before it starts shouting at you.

I love helping people in general but it is my calling to work with youth. I am very tuned in to this group of people and I seem to understand what makes them tick. I love it when they have an "a-ha moment"—when they finally understand themselves better. I love watching other people use the tools I have taught them; tools that help them feel valued in a society that, more often than not, makes them feel under-valued. And it is also important to me that I will understand more of what my own children have to go through because I have taken the time to work with youth and people in general.

One last area I think is important to touch on is keeping true to yourself by laughing and enjoying the moment (Chapter 8, Laughter is the Best Medicine). The times I am most stressed out, or the times I lose my perspective, are the times I am unable to keep laughing. We need to have belly laughs; great big, deep laughs where your stomach feels like it is going to explode if you don't stop. Being in helping careers, there are times when we really feel like crying. I know there have been many days where I felt I was vulnerable to depression because of the work we were doing. But by having a good laugh and being grateful for the positives in my life, I was able to see some light from dark situations. As Helpers, we need to cherish both the people we work with and the people we help; they are gifts given to us daily and we never know when we will come across that one person who is going to change us. All it takes is a thank you from a difficult client or a thoughtful gesture from someone who you least expected it from. I mention some personal examples in Chapter 10, The Gifts.

At the end of the day, what really matters in life is finding something you are passionate about and pursuing it—while maintaining balance. Learning appropriate balance is the key to having a successful life (more about this in Chapter 3, Creating Balance). When you feel balanced between your professional and private lives, your relationships with others—your partner, children, friends—will be stronger. Don't worry if your dreams change; we are all a work in progress. Having people who support you through your journey is the key. They don't even have to be a family member; you can be supported by a colleague, mentor or a close friend. For me, being able to come home at the end of a tough day to the support of my children and husband is absolutely priceless and I would not change those moments for anything in this world.

If you make sure that taking care of yourself first is your primary focus, then no matter what happens or what curve balls life tries to throw at you, you will be able to survive the roller coaster ride of ups and downs that is typical of working in any helping profession. Be sure to read the signs and know when enough is enough (Chapter 9, Knowing Yourself). Most importantly: remember to help others without losing yourself.

1

Respecting Yourself and Others

I always wanted to teach sixth grade. I often wonder now why I chose that particular grade. It may have been because I loved working with young children in the recreation field. But jobs were scarce when I graduated, and there were only a few positions available, at the high school level, so I felt fortunate to obtain employment. When I became a high school teacher my focus shifted to working with youth. I was nervous, but I was willing to try a new challenge.

The fear and self-doubt that go along with making big life changes are difficult and uncomfortable to confront, and that is precisely the time when we have to face them and work our way through them. I learned my fears about teenagers were unfounded—what a lot of wasted energy that was!—because the moment I started working with teenagers, I knew I was where I was meant to be. The job felt right and my intuition told me this was what I needed to do at this time in my life. It is a little hard to explain in words, but when we make a decision that is right for us, we get a feeling of confidence which is a result of knowing we are doing the right thing. This was how I felt after I started teaching high school.

Throughout your journey as a Helper, you may have times where you feel you lack confidence in your decisions. Don't let this get you down, but do learn from the feeling. Learn to trust yourself, but also learn to ask for advice and, more importantly, learn to listen to that advice when you need to. In this chapter we look at ways to respect yourself, to develop your self-confidence, to know when to ask for help, and to be genuine with your clients, students, patients, children—whoever it is you are helping. As Helpers we know that showing other people respect is an important quality, but we can get so wrapped up in their lives that we forget to respect and take care of ourselves.

Listen to Yourself

Everyone has an inner voice. It is important that we listen to what our gut or inner voice tells us. There have been times throughout my career that I have had to rely on my gut feelings to steer me in the right direction. It is almost like a sixth sense that we get. Listening to this inner voice can be vital, for example, when someone is melting down before our eyes, and we don't have time to consult a colleague or ask others for help. We need to be able to make split-second decisions, and our gut instinct can be a valuable guide in this process. If you work in the helping profession, you have been trained to do your job. Rely on your training to do the best you can and listen to yourself.

Other times we do not have to make split-second decisions. This is when we need to take the time to step back and reassess the situation. No one knows what is around the corner, so we can only go on our instincts. My instincts have taught me to respect others and myself. We teach people how we want to be treated and if we model respect for our clients, then we have set positive boundaries. We, as Helpers, also have to be genuine with our clients because people can see through the falseness. By being genuine, we help show our own self confidence and model a positive response in others. Finally, it is important for us as Helpers to learn from the lessons we are giving our clients. No one is perfect; we need to keep growing, learning and striving to do better. This can only help everyone in our lives—our clients, our families and friends and ourselves—in the long run.

You Are Responsible for How People Treat You

We teach people how we want to be treated. Sounds odd, maybe even backwards, but it is true. Pamela Butler wrote about this topic in her book, *Self-Assertion for Women*. She argues we can only teach people how we want to be treated if we learn to set limits for others. When we do not set these limits we are then being nonassertive and we are stating that our emotional needs are less important than other people's needs. Here, Butler shares this point in a discussion with someone in her therapy group:

> If I agree to accommodate my friends against my wishes, I feel resentful. This leads to shutting down my positive caring feelings for them, and I end up communicating to them, through subtle gestures, just the attitudes and uncooperativeness and unfriendliness that I was trying to avoid in the first place by not setting my limits.[4]

Butler goes on to talk about how women are especially bad at setting limits because we are used to giving up our identities to be helpful. She states,

> In our culture, women have been taught to be polite, to be unselfish, to subjugate their own needs to the needs of others. In playing out this culturally prescribed role, a woman can end up taking care of everyone but herself.[5]

This is not just the case for women; traditionally, women have done this more than men, but subjugating our own needs is something that some men do as well. We have to decide what is important to us and what we would like to spend our own time on. To be in control of our own destiny, we need to assert who we are. This means setting boundaries!

Dr. Philip McGraw (many of us know him as Dr. Phil) talks about this same concept in his book, *Life Strategies*. He breaks down life into ten "life laws" that will help you to live a fulfilled and gratifying life. His eighth life law is called, "We teach people how to treat us".[6] McGraw argues that people will treat you positively or negatively because your response to how you are being treated is working for them. That is, if the person you are dealing with does not get the desired responses, then their behavior will change. He goes on to discuss how relationships that show mutual respect between two people also abide by this law. For example, "If your partner treats you with dignity and respect, then it's only appropriate that you pay him or her off for that desirable behavior."[7]

Respecting Others for Their Unique Qualities

Not only do we need to set our own boundaries, but we need to model to others how we want to be treated. In the helping profession, we are role models for our clients. This is a strategy that works two ways: by making sure I teach others how I want to be treated, I also respect people for who they want to be. I have been able to look beyond the earrings, the attitudes and the tattoos. One of my biggest strengths when dealing with youth, and people in general, has been my ability to respect people for who they are in that moment of their lives. If we treat youth any differently than we would anyone else in our lives, then we are not being genuine and they will see right through us. This goes for adult clients too, old or young, whatever walks of life. People who are struggling are no different than you and I; they have just been going through some rough times. Granted the client or student does not have to be your friend—and should not be your friend if you are in a professional relationship—but you need to realize that if you, as an adult, do not give people respect, they will not give it back. It is amusing when adults try to act like teenagers to impress youth or young adults. They tend to look like they are not genuine. Acting your age and acting like yourself makes your actions more respectful in the eyes of youth and adults alike.

As Helpers we need to be cautious about our reactions to our clients because, let's face it, no matter what sort of profession you are in, people are seeing us because things are not going well for them. They have most likely faced a lot of negativity along their journey. Thus the more patience and respect we can show them in those moments when they are struggling, the more likely the desired changes will occur. Try not to focus on the outward appearance and mannerisms of the people you are helping—whether adult or youth—but instead focus on the inner work you as a Helper will be helping to produce with them.

Respect Yourself

What I did not immediately realize about respect was that I also had to respect myself. As I stated earlier about setting limits, you have to make sure you are taking care of yourself. By taking care of other people before my needs and by not respecting who I was and what I needed, I was projecting the image that everyone else was more important than me. Every Helper should repeat these words as often as necessary:

I am important

I value myself

I am valued by others

In the past, I made the mistake of forgetting this. I forgot who I was and what I needed. In essence, I was telling myself that I was not important; that my time was not valuable. In turn, I myself was not as valuable as everyone else. This way of thinking is wrong on multiple levels.

When do you know you have gone too far? How do you know if you are putting others first, before your own needs? Pamela Butler states that when we feel emotional stress or resentment toward those we are helping, we have gone too far in not getting our own needs met, and in letting others cross our boundaries.

For me, I can tell how tired I am, when I feel emotional stress and

I feel like I've been beaten up emotionally. It is when we feel like we don't want to go to work anymore. These are all signals that we need to be taking the time to rebuild our boundaries. It is time to step back and recharge our batteries.

Confidence can be a tricky thing. When a person lacks confidence, it can manifest in many ways and often it equates in our heads as "I am a loser." The worst part is, we can repetitively tell ourselves this every day and truly start to believe it. We can be our own worst enemy. We can, and often will, read negativity into situations, because this type of thinking is habitual.

Confidence can be projected. This is a great strategy when you don't feel confident, but you also need to internalize your body language. When you look on the outside like you have confidence, this may not be how you really feel! This may be how it looks but in reality we are melting away inside. Many people told me I was a very confident and awesome teacher and I would nod and thank them, but inside I couldn't believe it. In fact as a society people are lousy at taking compliments and this often signals a lack of confidence. At some point people need to learn to believe in themselves. Everyone should know how special they are. Thus as a Helper, you need to make sure you believe you are special and your clients or students are special too.

In my experience, girls tend to lack confidence more than boys. Although boys can have confidence issues, it just seems to be more prevalent in the girls I work with. Either way, when a person lacks confidence it can pour over in other aspects of their lives such as their demeanor when they walk into the door at the beginning of the day. That is why it is so important to not only give positive comments but to accept positive comments. When you are able to accept these positive, kind words and believe they are true, you have a chance of feeling more confident and acting that way. Try the challenge at the end of the chapter to see if you are able to accept compliments. You will be surprised how much more self-respect you will develop as a result.

Being Genuine = Personal Self-Confidence

The very first school I worked at was unique in the difficulties that we dealt with. Being a brand new teacher of teenagers was very stressful. So many parents were having a difficult time coping with their own lives, with little time or energy to help their teenagers. A lot of the students came from broken homes with families that had a long history of systemic problems we could not fix in the time we would spend with their children. But what was amazing and so rewarding was that any and all support and respect I gave the youth, they would give back in return. As long as I was genuine, they reacted positively towards me. Slowly, over the course of that year, I built up more confidence in my skills, and consequently in myself.

I will never forget at the end of that year when I was working with a particularly challenging group of grade ten students. They had been given consequences for some very negative behaviour on a field trip and afterwards there was some damage to my car. This was a low point for me. However, my success with one student changed what had been an overwhelmingly difficult day, into a day I could appreciate.

At the time, when students had a bad day or they struggled, I would give out caramel candies. That was one thing I became known for in the school. There was a young man that I met my first year teaching. He struggled in school with a learning disability, was very small for his age, and on top of all that, was not socially prepared for grade eight. His parents were very supportive and appreciated all the help we were able to give him. After learning about what had happened to my vehicle, he bought me the largest bag of these candies I had ever seen. He had earned some money doing chores and used that to buy the candies for me. He told me those should keep me going for a while. The fact that he had taken the time to do this touched my heart deeply. This student has always stayed with me, in a special place in my heart. These moments are so unexpected, they become the positive successes we as Helpers need to celebrate and hold close.

Knowing that I had inspired him in turn helped me do better in many facets of my life. The school administration and my colleagues all told me I was doing a great job, but I did not believe it until this teenager confirmed it. The first year of my career was not perfect; I made my fair share of mistakes and the learning curve was huge, but this young man showed me that I had given him enough respect that he wanted to give it back to me.

Upon further reflection today, I realize that after focusing on the successes I had that school year and building upon those, I was able to feel better about myself as a person. It is important to look at the mistakes we make and learn from them so we can continue to move forward and grow (I will expand on this concept in Chapter 6, Challenges Helpers Face). When something goes well in one aspect of our lives, it is amazing how confident we start to become in other areas of life. I began to feel better about many of my life decisions, and that was when I started to focus on positive choices.

After working at this school—even with some very difficult students—I felt pretty confident with my career choice, and with who I was becoming in my professional life. It was time to make some positive changes in my personal life.

I had always struggled with my weight and I used my increased self-confidence as the catalyst to lose weight. This was a decision I made for myself and not anyone else, and I think that is why I was successful—over eight months I dropped 85 pounds and looked the best I had ever looked in my adult life. It is amazing how confidence can bring about such positive changes. As Helpers, we need to remember that our jobs are part of our lives, but our jobs don't completely define us. We need to take care of ourselves and to keep our own level of self-worth healthy. Instead of letting bad situations drain us, we need to energize from the small successes. Working with high risk youth has given me so many gifts. One thirteen year-old who showed me I was making a difference in his life made all the difference to mine as well.

Don't Ride Other People's Roller Coasters

The feelings we have from these types of situations are why we become Helpers in the first place. Nothing can replace the adrenaline rush that comes from helping to facilitate change! Everyone in our profession has had this feeling, and this tends to be why we go back to work every day.

It is important to look at past successes, because life can be messy for everyone. Some people are born with more knocks against them. Remember we did not choose the life that these people did. As a Helper, you should not feel down because you have made positive choices in life. As well, you cannot feel guilty because you were born into a happy and positive family situation. The situations your clients and their families find themselves in may not be their fault but it definitely is not the Helper's fault. You cannot feel bad and take other people's problems on, and be successful over the long term. You will burn out, guaranteed. One of my colleagues once told me the key to working with people who have behaviour issues is to "not ride their roller coaster". In other words, they are going through some difficult times, but as a Helper you don't need to join them. In order to help, you need to stay calm and work with them through the skills they need to deal with their own lives. You really are just present to help with guidance.

Remember Yourself and Listen to Others

When you are trying to be genuine, the work needs to be about the client and not about yourself. You need to make sure your own issues are worked out before you take on someone who has a myriad of issues you are trying to help them with. Feelings have no time limit. It is essential for us as Helpers to deal with our personal negative feelings because otherwise, these feelings can creep up when we least expect them to. For example, a client discloses that they were assaulted in the park while walking home. To some of us this information, although distressing, is part of our daily work with clients. However, what if this same situation had happened to you personally? In that case, if your feelings about what happened in your own case are not dealt with, there is a danger that the work becomes more about you and not the client. There are times when we need to take a break from dealing with other people's problems and deal with our own. Listen to what your feelings are telling you.

Some years ago, I was dealing with some heavy emotional issues personally. My friend's son was terminally ill, work demands were high, and it was Christmas time, which is stressful in itself. Plus, a student had just told me about a horrible situation I could not help him with. I was feeling hopeless because there were so many obstacles that I could not help these people navigate and I was angry. I felt like a useless Helper. What was the point even working when I could not focus and my friend's family was suffering? Self-doubt was creeping in, in the worst way. If there is anything that I don't like in life, it is not being able to help people, because I am conditioned to help.

Then one of my co-workers did something that I had specifically asked him not to. I was mad, and I could not wait until the students left that day to tell this co-worker how I felt. I was going to take all my anger and frustration about everything that was going on out on this person because I was in a place of authority and I could. I was going to prove I was right and no one was going to stop me from doing this. I was ready to lay into him as soon as humanly possible.

I told another colleague about my plan. He let me talk it through and just as I was getting up to walk out the door he asked me to wait a minute. I was so angry and frustrated I did not want to wait but for some reason I listened. He asked me a simple question, "If you go out there and do this, who are you helping and what will it accomplish?"

When I paused, he knew that I was listening and then he carried on to ask, "If we are trying to focus on the positives and you state multiple negatives in a disrespectful way, how are we going to continue to achieve what we want in our program?"

I did not say anything but I did listen to what he said and thought about it. I really wanted to give this person a piece of my mind to let out all the pent up frustration. In the end, I decided to let it go.

I left and did not say a word to this person about it because it was not worth the damage. I was lucky that someone respected me enough to stop me and that I respected his opinion enough to listen. Other people have good suggestions, and when I look back at that moment, he was right. By listening, I resisted doing something that could have very easily done irreparable damage and accomplished nothing. It would have also created a defensive and most likely hostile working environment for days or weeks to come. The other thing I learned in that moment was how important it was to not talk to people when I was too emotional or angry. Those are the times that I can get myself into the most trouble and the damage sometimes can be, or has been, irreparable.

Hearing Advice

We all have emotions and it is natural that sometimes our feelings may get out of control, but taking our frustrations out on other people is not a healthy way of dealing with it. In my own way, I was asking for help in the first place when I told my colleague what I was going to do. By talking it through with him, I was able to get advice, hear the feedback, and act upon it.

When you struggle emotionally, it is important to surround yourself with people who can support you. If there is not a circle of people who can support you then you have to reach out and create one from friends, colleagues and/or professionals. This will be discussed in depth in Chapter 2, Asking for Help and Creating Support.

Developing Self-Care

As a Helper, you need to develop some form of self-care, and to do that you need to have a self-check system in place, especially if you are feeling frustrated and angry. What that looks like for each person will most likely be different. A couple of suggestions could be discussing difficult situations with a mentor, or not talking to people until the next day when you have calmed down or giving yourself some time to see a different perspective. In the helping profession things happen quickly and in those moments we have to do a lot of quick thinking. Thus if a topic does not feel good for you to discuss with people in that moment, don't do it then. Here's an example of an anger self-check list from a "20/20" video called *So Angry You Could Die*:[8]

1. Is this worth my attention?
2. Am I justified being angry about the situation?
3. Do I have an effective response?

If you answer "no" to any of these questions then you will most likely do more damage than good by getting angry with the situation. Plus this could, and most likely will, lead to trouble for you. When you think back to times when anger got you into trouble, you most likely would have answered no to one of the questions above. You need to figure out appropriate times to be angry and apply a positive response to this anger so positive results can happen. This is one way to keep yourself in check. Applying this method during moments of anger is one way you can stop yourself from making some big mistakes in your career and your life.

Internalizing Lessons Ourselves

It may be helpful when working on a structured lesson for an individual or a group that you work through the lesson you are teaching with yourself first. This is helpful for two reasons. Firstly, if you do the lesson, you can see where it may need improvement and secondly, you can look at past personal feelings that may come up.

Being able to handle what comes our way is a key to being successful in the helping profession. There have been times when I would be saying one thing to a student but in the same breath I am not believing or doing this myself. The old saying "Do as I say, not as I do." comes to mind. A common example of this is negative self-talk. Many people, including myself, have fallen into this trap from time to time.

An example was when I was working with a girl who thought she was not deserving of happiness even though she had finally found a job she loved. I was encouraging her to not feel this way, yet I was feeling the same way about myself. This has also been an issue for me when I have tried to lose weight. The only time I was successful with losing weight was when I had confidence and felt mentally prepared for the challenges that were ahead. It is important for you to feel good about yourself, and one way to promote this is through positive self-talk. We tell the clients we work with to do this every day but we tend not to do it ourselves.

Helpers regularly ask youth and adults to practice positive self-talk, but as Helpers we also need to look at ourselves. To help improve our positive self-talk, we need to look at the underlying reasons why we tend not to use it. For me, most of my negativity has stemmed from pain. I gained all my weight because I was in such gut wrenching grief over a family of relatives dying in a car accident at the hands of a drunk driver. I never wanted to go through that pain again. Somehow I thought that if I ate a lot and had an extra layer of fat on, no one would love me, thus I wouldn't have to worry about anyone being so close to me that I could lose them. In short, I ate to keep people at arm's length.

Although this now seems absolutely crazy, I truly believed my boyfriend at the time would not love me with the extra weight. Thus if he died I would never have to feel that excruciating pain again. However, protecting myself with fat only put huge strains on my health and my relationships at the time. When I finally gave up on this way of thinking, I was able to see that this may not be the best way to live. My boyfriend also did not scare easily. He fought to be a part of my life which made me realize this was not a healthy way to live and in order to enjoy my life I really needed to live my life. I am extremely happy he did not fall for such distorted thinking because I am happily married to him today. I was not respecting myself at that time, but I was lucky that other people reminded me that I deserved and needed to respect myself.

Pain Can Make Us Crazy

We do crazy things when we are hurting. And if you are hurting you are not in a position to help others. That is why it is so important to take care of yourself as much as you take care of others. As Helpers, we are human beings with feelings and emotions like everyone else. If we can focus on self-care then maybe we stay well-rounded and emotionally healthy. But this is an ongoing process. In my case, I need to constantly remind myself that keeping balanced and healthy is important for everyone involved in my life.

We chose this helping profession fully aware that our jobs can be difficult. Your family and friends likely did not choose this life for you. Thus at the end of the day, you need to make sure that other people in your life do not suffer from your choices. As a professional you have to be cognizant of this. Your family and friends did not choose for you to work long hours, and they did not choose for you to be unhappy when you return home from work. Part of making sure we take care of ourselves is making sure we are strong enough to deal with what our personal lives or families hand our way.

We are all striving to be the best we can be—to live in the moment and for the moment. Surround yourself with positive people and people who will keep you in check and will call you out when it is needed. Positive role models can be an integral part of having success in any field, but especially in our field, the helping field, where there is often no one right or wrong answer in the work we do. In the helping profession everything isn't black and white; just different shades of grey.

By making sure you respect yourself and who you are, you will have a higher personal success rate. The positive feelings will continue to shine through.

. . .

Points to Remember

- We all have an inner voice
  - Remember to listen to yours

- We teach people how we want to be treated
  - If we want people to respect us then we need to show them respect first

- We have to respect the people we work with for their unique qualities
  - We cannot judge them for how they look

- Respect yourself and your time
  - Set limits with your work and home life

- Learn how to accept a compliment (see the exercise below)

- Do not ride other people's roller coasters; you have enough on your plate already

- Pain can cause us to do crazy things
  - Try to stay in tune with yourself to make sure you are handling all of the information that is coming your way

Chapter 1 Challenge & Activity

1. Consider Compliments

Compliments are given out on a daily basis and it has taken me 20 years to accept them. When you are able to look at the positives in life, you feel better. This is true for others as well. Are you not trying to teach your clients that they need to feel better about themselves? So if you don't practice what you preach then you are not living the best life you can. Everyone in this world deserves to be happy and if you can accept the good and feel it inside and out, then your perspective on life becomes a whole lot better. You really do know more than most people give you credit for.

For the next week, instead of denying compliments or brushing them off, accept them and think about what that person is really saying. Remember there are many facets to confidence and being able to accept that others see good things about you is vital. It is amazing how much more powerful you feel when you believe positive words from others.

2. Anger and Self-Care Checklist

Think about the last three times you were angry. If this is too hard to remember, focus on the next three times you become angry. When you have calmed yourself down, ask yourself these three questions:

1. Is this worth my attention?
2. Am I justified being angry about the situation?
3. Do I have an effective response?

Once again, if the answer to any of these questions is "no" then this was not an effective way to deal with the situation and you needed to come up with a better alternative.

Keep a record of these situations (see worksheet Appendix A: Anger Questions Log). By looking at your answers you may begin to see patterns and areas you would like to change within yourself. Information can be powerful and acknowledgement, as we know, is the first part of change. You may find you need some outside support to help delve further into some issues. Being honest with yourself can only help you to improve who you are and how you can practice what you, as a Helper, preach.

2

Asking for Help and Creating Support

We don't become part of a helping profession because we want to make a lot of money, as there is not a lot of money to be had in this industry. Choosing a helping profession is usually about creating a life of integrity or fulfilling that part of you that genuinely wants to make a difference in the world. The problem Helpers face is we want to prove we can do the job as an independent professional, but we can get into trouble fairly quickly if we are not careful.

It is funny, as a learning support teacher I was always encouraging students to learn to ask for help when they needed it, yet when I had difficulties, I would rarely ask for help. Many students struggle with this task. Adults and professionals are no different. Most people find it difficult to ask for help because they fall into the stressful trap of thinking that they can handle it. You are not a weak person when you ask for help; you are just trying to navigate a system that is messy. You must recognize there are no perfect solutions to every problem that may arise with this work.

There are many aspects to look at when you are asking for help and creating support. First you need to learn to listen and be open to taking advice. People tend to get very defensive when it comes to listening, thus if you look at it from the perspective of enhancing the good work you are already doing, then it will help you to not shy away from finding some support. This chapter will explore why we tend to not ask for help and how you, as a professional, can get away from this thinking. Finally, we will look at natural role models and how to develop a successful support team.

When Personal Pride Gets in the Way

As stated previously, it is very important that you not only ask for help but that you are willing to listen to the answers or suggestions you are offered. It does not matter if you follow all suggestions, but they need to be considered. You just need to hear what that person has to say; you can adjust what they are saying to your own style or way of looking at things. When the person giving advice is not involved in the issue or situation, they tend to be more objective, which can help to give you a perspective you may not have thought of before.

One example of when I realized my pride got in my way of asking for help was when I was working in a district-wide department that was helping special needs students obtain work placements. My job was to guide others and create unique opportunities for this population of youth. It was one of the best jobs I had ever had and I was ready for the challenge. Toward the end of that year I got myself into a bit of a bind and I knew I should have asked for help but I felt I had something to prove being new, so I didn't.

One particular student was struggling and the school contacted me to help find a work or educational training placement for her. The family did not have any money and the young lady was ready to drop out of school. I had a meeting with a unique woman who was running a flower arranging program for an at-risk population of adults and she was willing to try placing the student in the program even though we did not have the funds to pay for the spot yet. Instead of running this by my principal, I took it upon myself to go full steam ahead and try to find some funds to pay for this. As well, the flower program administrator thought she should start and we would worry about the funds later. By the time I realized I was not going to be able to get the funds to pay for this program, it was too late. Plus, when

I asked for this student to be pulled out of the program, the instructor refused and told me that it was not fair to the student who was having success to pull her out now. When the principal finally got involved, the student now owed a lot of money. The flower program, even though I had asked them to withdraw her, demanded the district pay. I was in a muck of trouble.

If I had put ego aside and gone to the principal as soon as things had started to go off the rails or if I had taken a step back and tried to secure the funds first, then this would not have gone badly. I was so positive I would be able to fix the situation that I did not take the time I needed to make sure the details were worked out. Hindsight can give some great perspectives. Asking for help does not make you weak, it makes you smart.

The second time this happened I was working with another administrator. At the time, I was struggling with a staff member who did not like working with me and went out of her way to try to undermine my work. The administrator bluntly told me that I would have to be the one to leave the school. For a long time, I did not understand or agree with his opinion. The colleague who had issues with me blamed me for a lot of things and focused all of her anger towards me which made for a very stressful working environment. There are some things in life you can control but this one I couldn't. In teaching we are able to change jobs within a district and not lose seniority at the end of each school year. To do it mid-year is very difficult and can only be done in extreme circumstances. When I had the opportunity to go the first time, I did not take it because I was scared and dug in my heels. Why did I have to leave—why couldn't this other person leave? Two months into the next school year I finally understood. She was never going to leave so I had to for my own sanity. Now it was November and the school year had eight months to go. They were some of the longest months of my entire career.

The administrator kept telling me I needed to leave because this teacher would not and I did not listen. Had I listened, it would have ended the stress and would have caused less strain on my marriage and working relationships with other colleagues. What I learned from this situation is to always consider what someone else has to say. By the time I was ready to listen it was too late. If I had been willing to listen earlier, then I would not have suffered so many negative days. I was finally ready to leave, but I had to stay for the remainder of my contract.

Be Open to Suggestions

Weigh your options and make an informed decision; this will help to avoid falling into a similar trap. As well, don't let personal pride get in the way of listening to what other people have to say. They just may have some good ideas or have thought of some things that you had not.

This administrator became one of my mentors when I had issues with students to work through and this was very helpful. When I finally made the decision to leave the school, I told him first. I know that he knew I needed to go but he stood up and gave me a hug and stated that he would miss me. His voice cracked. These small moments you share with positive people in your support network over the course of your career are precious. These moments should be treasured for many years to come. These are also the moments that help us grow and change.

As Helpers, we really need to make decisions considering all information, not just part of it. We don't have to listen to people when they give advice, but being willing to hear what they have to say is important. We forget that our bubbles can be popped when we least expect it. Ego can get in the way but if we try not to let it then we are better off. Making decisions with all the information in front of us is the only way we can move forward in life and at work. This is when the best decisions are made.

Breaking Down Barriers

People who create a barrier between management and staff are not doing the workplace justice. Sure, there are times when they are separate. However, you need to remember both groups have the same end goal—to help people. You need to make sure you take care of one another because no one else will. At the end of the day, you can only control yourself. Having people there to help you can be a blessing and make you feel you are not alone when it comes to making tough decisions both personally and professionally.

There are times when protocol is important, especially when you are trying to solve problems that have no easy answers. More times than not, management will think better of you for coming to them for input around difficult decisions. Administrators or managers often are put in a different category and you feel you will look like you are incompetent if you ask for their support and help through tough times. This is not true, especially since they were put in charge based on their experience, and the problem will fall on them if things go wrong. Going to them in the first place may stop some unneeded displeasure down the road.

The question I have about our profession is why we seem to shy away from asking for help. John Grohol made some interesting observations about this question—he believes we are afraid to look too vulnerable or we don't know enough about our job to realize that it is not frowned upon to ask for help:

> I think the number one reason why people don't ask for help is simply **fear**. Fear that others will judge them for seeking help, fear that others will see them as weak or damaged. This fear is the same kind of fear that holds many people back in their lives.
>
> But fear, like any emotion, can be overcome. It takes effort and work, but if you conquer this fear, you can seek out help and improve your life or situation.[9]

Maybe our issues do go back to fear and how we may look like we don't know what we are doing. We need to have more confidence in what we do and if we ask others for support and help, then it will make us look better not worse.

I know the times that I did not ask for help got me into trouble. I have learned valuable lessons at my own expense. Do you feel some days you are just banging your head against the wall trying to move forward on your lonely ship and if you had just listened to someone or been willing to listen, life would have been better? Those first few years in a new job are brutal. You are trying to learn the position and understand what needs to be done and you can be so overwhelmed it feels like you are drowning. The smoother the path can be for you, the better, and that is why having a mentor or role model can be very helpful.

Natural Role Models

Let's face it, you are going to be a role model for others whether you want to or not because once you start working with the public, and they see you in your community, you will naturally assume that role. If you live your life with integrity then you will have no difficulties doing this. A good friend of mine told me if you can look in the mirror at the end of your day and you are happy with who you see and with the decisions you made during your day, then you have done well. I really aspire to continue to make sure I can be happy with myself and the decisions I make each day.

I am a firm believer that you cannot emulate real life in a classroom or office—that is why when you teach people life skills you need to take them into public in real situations to practice them. When working with intellectually disabled youth and adults, my team takes them on regular community outings to teach life skills. This was the best decision we made and it is where some of our most important work has been accomplished. As a group, we try different sports or activities that we had never participated in before. Sometimes we were horrible—for me that was rock climbing, horseshoes and basketball—but we still were out there together trying to learn. What we, the staff, were modeling, was trying and enjoying different activities, without worrying too much about how good we were or how good we looked. As Helpers, our anxieties were raised just like our students' were, and this was a fantastic way to show that we all deal with the same issues and to role model how we work through anxiety in different situations.

Adults, who looked like they had it all together, became so proud in front of the students when they conquered their fear of heights and got to the top of a climbing wall, or tried new sports that made them anxious; these efforts were well worth it. It was our real-life opportunity to teach appropriate reactions to situations we could not have emulated in the classroom. In the end, we had fun as a group experiencing these new activities, and the students had an opportunity to work with adults and teach them a few skills along the way.

Seeking Appropriate Help

Every time I've changed jobs or been promoted, I've had an opportunity to develop new skills and build on the ones I already had. At the beginning of any new situation, life can be very overwhelming, and this is the time we need to admit we don't know everything and to seek out help when necessary.

One time, I was working with students who had cognitive disorders and difficulties controlling their behaviour. This is a very challenging group because they cannot always put cause and effect together right away. I will never forget when my mentor called and asked how things were going and I told her after the first two days I was ready to quit. I honestly felt like I was never going to make it through another minute with these students. I remember wondering what in the world I had gotten myself into. This particular class could not curb their profanity for one second and they did not understand how to act appropriately in public. Another big obstacle was that no team had been established yet to help support these individuals!

I met with my mentor, who had many years of experience working with cognitively disordered behaviour students, and she was someone I trusted a great deal. When she asked me how it was going, I was honest and told her I hated it, that it was turning out to be the worst experience of my teaching career and I was precariously close to quitting. After she let me vent she pointed out that students don't have to solve all of their problems in one day and we don't expect them to. She challenged me to ask myself why I was trying to solve all their problems at once. I had never thought about this. Then she asked what the worst behaviour was—the one behaviour that bothered me, as a professional, the most. I replied, the swearing. So she suggested we play a game to help with changing the behaviour.

At this point I was willing to try anything. The next day we played a game called Red Light, Green Light. This game is usually played in a gym and it is similar to the running game Go, Go, Stop. Here's how it works: the students are allowed to swear and say anything they want for one minute. This is the "green light". Then when the light is red, they are not allowed to use any profanity for 20 minutes. Of course, we would have rewards and incentives to help them stick to their plan. Well, I must tell you, did I ever learn some choice phrases! But over time the "red light time" of no swearing would increase each time until, finally, one day we got through the whole class without swearing.

As many people who work in our field know, one cannot change a behavior without helping to find a replacement behavior. So the other aspect that was important was to give the students more appropriate replacement words to use. Brainstorming this with the students and leaving them posted on the classroom board helped the students develop the desired replacement behaviour. My mentor also made some suggestions of other activities I could implement. I could not believe it when they worked. I was hooked. She mentored me and slowly guided me so we could initiate some basic behaviour changes and develop a more manageable class. This would not have happened had I not been able to ask for help!

Willingness to Hear Others

Having the ability to listen to what my mentor had to say created an environment of success in that program. There is no "I" in team, and over and over again I have personally been reminded of that in my life. When you have a great team, then you have a great program. The next year I had a teaching partner who brought new skills to the table and together we were both able to navigate the work issues we faced every day. It has been both a joy and pleasure to have a great teaching partner and to develop into a strong team. We work hard to make each other look like a hero at the end of the day and there are many pieces to the puzzle that came into play to make this work.

Joel Zeff calls this "Team Effectiveness" in his book, *Making the Right Choice*. He discusses ways to develop a team approach in both business and life. His suggestions are based on two principles:

1. Take responsibility for your role and do the best job possible.
2. Help everyone else achieve success.[10]

Zeff believes that if you do what is expected of you, and you follow the appropriate guidelines while working as a team, you will be able to have success. In other words, if you do your job well but one of the team members is not working well, then the entire team will be let down. However, if you build a team and work to help each other out to ensure success, then everyone feels positive and in return, the team will be successful. It is a different way of looking at teams and one that can only enhance the work you are doing with your organization. He does stress that if you make the teamwork complicated then no one will win. Keep things simple and by taking your time and working through the problems together, success will be on your side.

Surrounding Yourself with Success

Successful work begins with a positive team. The most pleasure and success I have had was when I was part of a team who dealt with students together. One cannot always have this type of environment but when you get an opportunity to work with a phenomenal team, take it. There were times when two people talking to a student would lead to more success because we each had a different approach. Each person can bring different skills and insights to the conversation.

Developing teams with some of your good role models can be very helpful. I have had role models and mentors throughout my career and still do. If you believe you have mastered your craft then I am here to tell you there is always something new for you to learn. If you have a wealth of experience, this can only enhance the team and bring forth valuable information for all the people on the team. Don't forget, there are always new theories being developed, so someone fresh out of university may have had some opportunities to find new approaches or unique ways of trying activities. In other words, everyone has a contribution to make so consider that before you act like the expert.

Life can throw everyone a curve ball or two. The best way to deal with these situations is to have good role models and a strong positive team to help navigate. Progress may be slow but it will come.

Once, my teaching partner and I were working with a student who was having a bad day, and consequently, the student was in a low mood. I had never seen a student that low before in my entire working life. Luckily both of us, my colleague and I, were there because we were using different approaches to try to help this student work through his difficulties.

My teaching partner is a trained professional counsellor whom I really admire and I have learned many great counselling techniques just from watching him work. He seems to understand which questions to ask next and how to develop a trusting relationship with people. When he ran out of ideas in the moment, I used some of the tools I had learned over the years. Generally your ideas will come from (as we saw in Chapter 1) gut instincts in the heat of the moment. Being in this work you most likely have learned many skills along the way—don't hesitate to use them. There is no set way to work with anyone and what we have to remember as professionals is when something does not work, try something else or seek out other sources and suggestions.

This day we both used our different skill sets and talked this student out of his dark hole. It was such a relief when one of our strategies worked and the student started talking about what was going on for him. You can imagine our relief because the last thing you want to do is have to seek hospitalization for someone. We can develop our skills further or give them tune-ups but the bottom line is that sometimes you are just relying on that training to move forward. This can be an overwhelming experience. We make a phenomenal team and I was sad when we decided we needed to move on to different work because I knew these powerful results we had created as a team would be over. This is a case of where as a team we truly accomplished more than we would have separately; I really cherish that time that I got to work so closely with him.

The Power of the Debrief

Debriefing is an important part of working with clients. This is an opportunity to go over what worked well and build upon this positivity for future cases. In the previous situation when we debriefed, my partner/mentor told me he thought I had used some pretty good counselling skills and came up with some unique ways to try to help this student. This was one of the best compliments he could have given me because I always believe that he is the expert and when he told me this it meant the world to me. This is another example of how a team can help keep your spirits up and help each other develop better skills. It also demonstrates that giving compliments about good work can help boost self-worth. It also shows we are comfortable asking for help. A comfortable environment can only help the team become stronger in the long run.

One of the positive ways to debrief is to use what is called Appreciative Inquiry. This is where you focus on positive methods or strategies and continue to build upon them when working in business, education, counselling or individually in any field. This is based on a philosophy that when we ask negative questions we are asking for negative responses. Thus the same should be true for positive questions; they create a more positive frame of mind. The hope is to envision a positive future or relationships with others by building upon successes.[11]

Keys to a Good Team

How do we develop successful teams? What do we look for when we look for a mentor, role model or a professional partner? To develop a successful team you do not have to pick the people that are exactly like you, but it would be helpful if the team has the same underlying philosophy. Choosing the appropriate team will help give different insights, great wisdom and support for decisions that are made with all the information gathered. That does not mean the person in charge is not responsible for the decisions made in the end, it means that having a variety of input makes the person in charge better informed or educated and it can make decisions easier to make.

On a more personal level, everyone needs a circle of support. If I did not have the strong circle I have around me, then many of the horrible issues I have to deal with daily would not get solved. When I have questions, I reach out and ask. When I am dealing with crazy situations I am trying to navigate, I reach out and ask. When I am suffering, I reach out and talk. The circle does not have to be very big; it just has to be chosen well.

How to Choose a Team

Think about the areas of life or work you are challenged in, that give you stress, or where problems don't seem to be getting resolved. Could you use help in these areas? In my own case, I identified three areas—my mental health, work-related issues and my overall physical health. Let me break down each area and explain why they are all so important.

1. Mental Health

Mental health is important because, in the helping profession, we are often dealing with people's raw emotions. We are all human and it can be hard to remember that this is your work life, not your life. Often the people we are helping have significant baggage of their own and at times it is difficult to remember their baggage or problems are not our personal baggage too. As Helpers, we can delve into some deep wounds and be exposed to some pretty horrible things and we need to personally process them too. The first person I recommend you choose for your circle of support is someone who will listen to your issues and help guide you through them on a confidential level so you can work through any personal emotional issues that may come up during your life at work.

When you feel your needs are not being met through your own support system, it is important to remember it is not a bad thing to talk to a psychologist or counsellor who can help you sort out your own feelings without you breaching the confidentiality of the people you help. Speaking to a professional, you are entitled to have a non-judgmental environment and the sessions are confidential.

Sometimes, as Helpers, we resist the idea of receiving help ourselves. But you need to remember that while your clients are going through these issues you are lending them your emotions and support too. You may have thick skin, but the issue is still there for you to deal with. At times, having a job in the helping profession can really be a burden. When I first started teaching I did not understand why we were always provided with free counselling services—now I do. This work is not easy. It will bring up past experiences that are extremely difficult for a person to deal with, but with proper support one can not only make it through, but at the end be recharged and ready to move forward and help the next person in need. For more information on how to access professional counselling, please see Appendix B.

2. Work-Related Mentor

When dealing with people's emotions or behaviour, no one has all the answers. The best team I ever worked with always talked about different philosophies that may help with specific students or clients. There is so much material out there that it is hard to narrow down or pinpoint one specific way of dealing with an issue. Remember every person fits a different mold. One philosophy will not work for everyone. A work-related mentor can help bring new ideas, strategies, and/or philosophies to the table. So having a mentor help guide you or to bounce ideas off of is key to a positive and successful working environment.

Work-related issues are tough. As a Helper you are trying to help guide people through some pretty horrible situations that they can find themselves in. There have been times when I have worked with people who are so upset about their situations (and have every right to be) that they cannot see the light at the end of the tunnel. Everything is bleak and grey. Making sure you have tried a multitude of strategies can only help. There are experts all around you; try to use them! Collaborate on ideas that can possibly help with your clients/students. It can only enhance your work.

3. Personal Health Support

Finally, the last person on my team is someone who helps me keep my personal health in line. I have someone who will listen when things are rough but who, just as importantly, also helps teach me what type of exercise program I should be following and what I should be putting into my body. Food is an important aspect of life as it keeps you going when you are tired. It will also make you feel energized in a day, especially the tough days when your energy can be drained by the type of work you do. So having the proper exercise and nutrition program can only help you.

During stressful days, just remember you don't have to work on personal and work issues alone. If you need some human contact to help you get through your day then take it. If it means you need to remember the good times with reminders all around you, then create it. Just remember to cherish the moments because before you know it, there will be another roller coaster ride that you may end up getting yourself on. One of the keys to success is trying to keep yourself balanced personally, professionally and in check with your family. Creating this balance will be explored in the next chapter.

Points to Remember

- Learn to listen
  - You don't have to follow all suggestions
  - Other people can contribute good ideas
  - Be open to the possibilities

- Break down barriers at work
  - Bosses/managers can be approachable and usually have more experience
  - Use their expertise to your advantage

- Develop a good team—they will
  - Give different insights
  - Have great wisdom
  - Help support your decisions
  - Look at three areas for your team:
    1. Mental health
    2. Work-related issues
    3. Physical health

Chapter 2 Challenge & Activity

1. Personal Networking

Look at the people you network with (see Networking template in Appendix C). Choose three to five people in each of the four areas who will support and help you through tough decisions. Discuss with each individual if they would be interested in working with you on different aspects of your life such as personal, professional, exercising, taking care of yourself, etc. You will be amazed how many people you know and how quickly people are willing to help one another out. You may also want to share your experiences with a friend or family member; there may be more similarities between what you and they are going through than you realize.

2. How Daily Decisions Affect You Personally

Here is something for you to try to see if you can live with the daily decisions you make and how they may affect your views on your job and your life. For one week, write down ten decisions you have made. Use two different columns; put the positive decisions in one column and the negative decisions in another. After one week, if you have more positives than negatives, you are doing pretty well.

If you want to build on your positives, then you need to accept the good you are doing and not dwell on the negative decisions. The goal is to improve and grow. Building upon your positive experiences usually leads to positive growth. Use what is working; this will help you to move to the next level of personal growth. This is the premise of Appreciative Inquiry. See the template in Appendix D for this exercise.

3

Creating Balance

When I think of balance what springs to mind is someone walking on a tightrope or across a balance beam. We all walk a tightrope when trying to figure out what is our best course of action when it comes to work, life and recreation. I have found that throughout my working life, there are times when I am out of balance. Incidentally, those are the times I have either gained weight or barely maintained the weight I was at. Also, those were the times when I would hurt myself working out or get very sick. My body was telling me I was not maintaining the balance I needed.

In this chapter we will explore how work does not define who you are—you do. We are going to try to understand what balance really means by looking at how we manage our time and how we can keep ourselves motivated to stay on track. Another area we will look at is how we communicate with others and what role we play when things don't work out. Finally, it is important to understand parameters with all of our relationships and we need to make sure we are finding the right balance and setting aside time to recharge our batteries.

Work Does Not Define You

It is important to have a life outside of your job. Many times we get caught up in our work world where we want to feel valued and appreciated but forget about what we valued about ourselves before we became employed in this career. When I think about my job, I realize I am very good at what I do, but what I do has caused a lot of stress for me at times. So how are you able to spend your day dealing with lots of people, then go home to be a parent, wife or friend, find time to do daily chores, exercise and relax? I am exhausted just thinking about my multiple "to-do lists".

A great resource that deals with the multiple activities we have to do in a day is the book, *Time Management from the Inside Out* by Julie Morgenstern. She discusses ways to figure out why we may feel like we have completed nothing in our day. Morgenstern suggests that time management and struggles with organization go hand-in-hand. Her book offers reasons as to why your life may be not working for you and gives you strategies to develop your own time management skills.

At the beginning of the book she suggests we look at how we spend our time and analyze this for at least three weeks. This will give some insight into what our time is spent on. Then Morgenstern wants you to look at your motivation for how you are dividing up your time and ways you can improve on your time commitments based on what you value the most.

> We each have different needs at different points in our lives. There may be a time in your life when work takes precedence over everything else; another period when family becomes your priority.[12]

Julie Morgenstern goes on to discuss how we have a tendency to stand in our own way and we need to be aware of this. We need to look at what we may be doing to stop ourselves from having success. What is great about her book is she has a nice way of laying out problems and solutions. She recommends a three-step program: analyze, strategize then attack. Morgenstern suggests this method will prepare you for success with time management and if you can successfully develop your time management skills then life in our busy world will become easier to manage.

What Is Balance?

So what is balance? I believe we need to have cohesiveness in all aspects of our lives to make sure we are able to cope with other people's situations. When I think of my life I break this down to four simple categories—work, personal ("me time"), exercise and family.

Work Time

Everyone has a source of work—stay at home mom, going out to work outside of the home, working from your home—whatever your situation is, we all have some form of work. The trick to working is to not let it spill over into your personal life. Sometimes it can when you have special projects due or a major deadline is looming, but making sure it is the exception and not the norm is the goal. You not only need to find balance in your life in general, but you also specifically need to find balance at work. Maybe this means you cut back on your hours if you cannot fit everything in or maybe this means you don't take your briefcase home with you every day. Whatever that may look like for you, finding a balance between personal and professional life is important. Take a step back and reassess what you want to do; maybe that means you don't talk about work from 5 pm on Friday until 8 am on Monday morning. Looking at ways to be able to walk away from a situation is the best way to ensure you have balance within your work life versus your home life.

In *Simplify Your Work Life,* Elaine St. James discusses the common mistakes we make when it comes to work and how, if we take a step back and look at what we are doing to ourselves, we may find that our very stressful jobs are not necessarily making us happy. Interestingly, she argues that instead of working longer hours to correct the problems, working fewer hours will help to increase your productivity and your overall morale about work. When her life was out of balance it became way too complicated and that is when she took a step back. St. James states that she thought she was working for money but in the end she realized she was:

> ... most productive, most committed, most happy, and most financially rewarded when I love the work I do. So, contrary to what some may believe, simplifying is not about retreating to a cabin in the woods and leading a dull, inactive existence. Rather, cutting back your hectic work pace gives you the opportunity to make sure that you're doing work you love.[13]

Making sure that your work life is in balance creates stability and enjoyment for the work you are doing. It will also help give you inner peace and make you feel like your life is doable even when it seems to get chaotic and busy. Getting paid to do a job you love is what we all need to strive for in life because then the job is not a chore; it is what makes life exciting when you get up every morning. Isn't that the key to life? To find your passion and strive to get paid for doing something that does not feel like work?

Personal Time

When you have had some adversity in life you tend to cherish every moment you have in your personal life. It also helps you to focus on the importance of developing a network and social life outside of the work place. If I was to only go to work and come home that is not an existence that would continue to bring me joy and happiness. This does not mean we cannot be friends with the people we work with; it means we want to make sure we also have friends and activities outside of the workplace. If we remember what brings us joy and go out and do that both professionally and personally, life will seem a whole lot more in balance.

In my case, I have many hobbies and interests. Most of them are physical at the moment because trying to fit everything in can be difficult with family and household obligations. I make sure I take the time to go to the gym to exercise a minimum of two times per week with a trainer. I really love swimming so I joined a swim club twice a week. Curling is another sport I used to do when I was young and just came back to recently. I love that the season is only six months long so it does not get in the way of other sports that interest me. I was able to find activities I enjoy that also help to keep me active, both mentally and physically. So I am not only carving out personal time, I am making sure I stay true to my physical health.

Exercise

Sometimes people find it hard to be motivated or don't feel they have the time to commit to all of this intensity. I tend to agree. At times it is really difficult to keep the motivation going, especially when you don't see results. It is important to remember you cannot see results inside your body or your brain. These areas you are helping just by making sure you exercise. Looking beyond the frustration and keeping your focus in the long term will pay off.

Remember why you are doing the activity in the first place: you are trying to relax and enjoy yourself, with the overall goal of better health. Throughout my journey, the one thing I figured out is no matter how I look, exercise helps me with stress and is healthy for my body. You don't have to have a perfect body to prove you are exercising.

The trick to exercising is to find something you like to do—does this sound familiar? When I started to lose my motivation for going to the gym, I decided to enter a race to have something to train for. Since I made this decision, I have competed in sprint triathlons, relay triathlons and open water swim races. These events gave me the motivation I needed to push through the training. My goals for racing are to continue to improve my own times and to have fun. It is important to remember to focus on your own personal goals, whatever those are, during a race. As well make sure you have a good time while trying something new and exciting. The feeling you get when crossing a finish line and seeing all the people there cheering for you (no matter what place you are in) is amazing!

Other people need motivation in other forms. If money is an issue, be creative in achieving your goal. You can look for a volunteer at the gym to help train you or volunteer time yourself or even try the bartering system. I did that for a while with my trainer because having to pay a lot of money up front can be difficult and hard on the budget. If you really want something enough, you just have to think creatively to obtain it.

See the Challenge at the end of the chapter for an exercise in how to find or rediscover activities you enjoy.

Taking Time with Family

Family time is another area that, if applicable to you, you need to set daily time aside for. As a Helper, I see too many families that struggle with trying to make ends meet who are working so hard to put food on the table that sometimes they feel they don't have the energy to do anything with their children. I find this very sad, as children appreciate attention and shared experiences, neither of which cost money. Life is too short and children grow up too fast for you to let this time slip away.

Time can be difficult to carve out because everyone has activities they are doing and everyone is busy. In our house we are very lucky; we have created an environment where one spouse works outside of the home and one works from home. We both have to work to maintain the lifestyle we have chosen but for me, being a teacher means getting a great deal of time off during the year to spend with my kids. When activities get busy and our schedules seem crazy, we still manage to find family time for games night or activities we can do together. There always seems to be an end to the craziness when we will have more time to spend with our kids. Any time you can spend with your family, even when they are adults, is time well spent and it can be the best cure for a bad day at work!

There are many lessons we can learn from our parents, close family members or even our friends' families. A lesson I learned from my family, which I mentioned earlier, is having dinner together as a family. Sometimes work schedules don't allow this so it may not be feasible every day, but do it as often as possible. Pick a night that everyone is free and sit down to a meal. This is a precious time for the family to communicate with one another and learn what happened during their day. Communication is a key to keeping on top of what your family is going through. Talking to your children at dinner will open the door to easier communication when the time comes, and your children need your guidance. Communication skills are important to have and model to your clients as well.

Don't Beat Yourself Up

There have been many times during my career when I have felt like I was letting my children down. I was spending way too much time focusing on activities I was doing for work and not enough time focusing on my children. I would get stressed and feel like I was ignoring my kids. My life was a little out of balance but I knew that once a big project was over, life would get back to normal. My kids once asked why I wasn't taking them to school and picking them up or why I could not attend many activities that were held during the school day. As a working mother it would hurt me to the core when I had to miss these events. My husband was so wonderful because he told them I get to spend extra time with them at Christmas, spring break and two months in the summer. That was my extra time with the kids. He made them feel so much more important than I had at that moment. I do make sure I spend most of my holidays with my children.

Work is part of us but it shouldn't define us. At the end of a long bad day, a hug can send all your troubles away and for me a hug from my children is the best part of my day.

Communication Is the Key to Strong Relationships

When I think back through the years from when I first met my husband to today, I realize we have been through a lot together. Although we look like we have it all together, there have been times when I was worried the relationship was not going to make it. One of those times, years ago, my husband was having a rough time and he wasn't a very happy person. He had not found a career choice he liked yet, he felt adrift, and he started taking his frustrations out on our relationship. At first this would happen in subtle ways, arguing points until he felt he was right or picking apart how I would parent the kids. We had agreed when we first had kids, that agree or not, we would not interfere with what happened when the other was disciplining our children, that instead we would discuss it behind closed doors afterwards. This scenario would create a united front and make for some lively discussions in the bedroom at night.

With this rule being broken and him being angry and sad a lot of the time, things began to get very strained. Our communication was going down the tubes because it was easier to ignore the problem than to deal with it. I want to point out I was not fully innocent in this either. Although my life was a little better structured at the time, I let him go down a path that was not nice for either of us. I let him take his frustrations out on me when I would not have let anyone else do that to me. As I stated earlier, we teach others how to treat us and I was not talking or trying to find out what was bothering him. Reflecting back, I think I was scared of what may be around the corner and it was easier to ignore the issue than deal with it.

So what to do? I chose to continue to ignore the problem until we almost got to the point of no return and separation was on the table. When the children started to notice he was angry and sad, I realized we needed to do something about this situation together. Work needed to be done on the relationship as much as he needed to work through some things personally.

Ignoring this problem was a mistake and the lesson I learned in my situation was that my husband needed some help and by the little things he did and said, he was actually asking me to help him. I was ignoring all the signs. At work I could see signs of difficulties with others but I was not present enough for my husband. I had also helped make him angry because I knew how to push his buttons so there were times when I would provoke him. I had to own that and stop my negative behaviour. He needed some guidance on where to go because he did not mean to be angry and frustrated. There were parts of him that were out of balance and together we needed to repair ourselves, then the relationship. The most important thing I needed to do was to make sure I communicated what I needed out of the relationship and owned what I was responsible for causing. Finally, I needed to have patience because change is difficult and we need to give our loved ones the time and space to process and implement change.

Our biggest stumbling block was our lack of communication. I am a Helper and it was so embarrassing that I was not willing to listen and push the conversation we needed to have. We were also avoiding each other because it was easier to deal with our lives in vacuums than to admit we needed help. In the end, we spent a short period of time apart and started communicated through computers and texting. For the first time in a very long time, we began to talk about everything and started saying the things that needed to be said. All of that unspoken stuff came pouring out of each of us.

As well, when we were apart we worked through a lot of our own personal issues. It actually seemed easier to do when there was a bit of space so that individually we could work through things. I am so happy we chose to fix our marriage instead of giving up on it. However people decide to work on their relationships—through group work, professional counselling, time apart, buying a workbook to work through issues—it is vital to find the strategy that is best for them. Just remember there is no easy fix and if one way does not work, be willing to try something else. Or, you may have to work through the relationship in multiple ways.

It is important to keep in mind that there are two people in a relationship and the way this relationship is worked on needs to be a mutual decision. When you have adversity in your relationship it is amazing how much better the other side can be when you work through it to a positive place—my husband and I are living proof of this. So try not to be scared of relationship or personal work because the work just might end with a positive resolution.

Some suggestions on ways to find support for a relationship and books on the subject are listed in Appendix E.

Parameters Need to Be Set

Many positive outcomes came out of our relationship work. My husband and I decided to implement a few rules for our relationship. One was that we would make sure we spoke to each other every day at night after the kids were in bed, but before we went to bed. We were making sure to carve out communication dates and/or times.

Secondly, if we were apart for any reason—work trips or recreational sporting events, we would continue to communicate through text or email every day. God bless technology so that it is easier to keep in touch with one another.

Finally, it was important for us to have regular date nights. We made sure that once a week, for a minimum of two hours, we would spend some time together. Sometimes it is as simple as making dinner for two and sitting down and discussing our week with one another. Other times it is a special recreational activity or evening out to go to a show. It doesn't matter what we do, what matters is spending time together. We have to set aside time to work on our relationships. Eventually our children will be grown up and will move out and if you don't make sure you have some life carved out or set up before they leave you will have nothing to look forward to. Don't get me wrong, I love my children and I love spending time with them, but I also love my husband and want to make sure I spend some time with him.

If you are not in a relationship with anyone significant, that does not mean you cannot make time for people who mean something to you. For example, take the time to book a coffee date with a friend you haven't had time for lately, but want to reconnect with. It is amazing how we get so busy with our lives that we can forget others. There may be a family member you have not seen in a long time. The best way to keep track and make sure you hold yourself accountable is to book an appointment with yourself. It usually does not take long before you are looking forward to this special time with family or friends.

Find the Time for You

A friend once told me to stop and smell the roses—when you take the time to think about that it is very profound. Many people do not take the time to relax and sit back from their life. Take 30 minutes a day to read a book or do some yoga stretches. For me, swimming is like meditation. I find when I am swimming I am not only exercising but I am also relaxing my brain and my thoughts—a tried and true way for me to deal with stress.

An area of life we don't tend to take the time to work on is our relaxation time. For me, after a long day at work I like to exercise, then spend dinner time with my kids and try to relax in the evening. I am very good now about not taking work home with me. When you work full time it is very difficult to not spend every waking hour catching up. If there is anything I have learned it is that the work will always be there and it may never get done, but if you wear yourself out over working then eventually it will affect your ability to do your job.

So how much relaxation time do we need? I think it depends on the person. I don't think there is a magic formula: for some people it may be as simple as taking that moment to look at a sunset, for others it may be a planned road trip and taking in some special sites and places you have always wanted to see. Or it could be to schedule time to relax in your favourite chair and read a book for pleasure. The beauty of relaxation time is that it is specific to your needs and not about what other people think. This is a time to help you individually recharge your batteries in whatever way will work for you.

However you find balance in your life, you need to find it. Making sure to have balance will help you stay healthy and focused at work as well as in your personal life. Don't be afraid to try a range of activities to help find the ones you like. Think of it in the same way as reading books. There are millions of books written in this world. If you don't like what you are reading then don't read it, because you will never get to every book. It is the same way with activities. If you don't like an activity or it does not help you relax than maybe it is time to try something else. When you are willing to try a variety of activities, you never know what you may find you enjoy doing and helps you to relax a bit more. It will be time well spent.

. . .

Points to Remember

- ▸ Work does not define you
  - − Find work that will bring you joy

- ▸ There are four categories of life balance:
  - − Work
  - − Personal
  - − Exercise
  - − Family

- ▸ Don't beat yourself up if life is not perfect
  - − That is what makes life so interesting!

- ▸ Learn how to effectively communicate
  - − Set parameters and rules with communication
  - − It will only strengthen each relationship

- ▸ Make sure you are taking care of yourself
  - − You are the most important person in your life

Chapter 3 Challenge & Activity

1. Activities We Enjoy

Think back to a time when you felt alive, or about an activity that gave you pleasure as a child—something that would bring you great joy. Write down what you were doing or the activities that made you feel this way. Replicating today the positive joyful feelings you had as a child or young adult is what we are trying to focus on for this challenge. There are no set rules on how you decide to shape your spare time, so try to capture the excitement and good feelings you once had by choosing activities that will bring you this happiness again.

Another idea is to ask a group of friends to try a new activity each month so you are spending time with friends but also spending some time doing something that may bring new pleasure into your life. Just like a book club will try to read a new book each month, you are going to try a new activity each month individually or as a group. This gives you an opportunity to maybe find something you are good at or want to pursue further as a regular activity. So the challenge is to find activities you enjoy doing and make time to do them every week. Finding activities you enjoy and that bring happiness to your life will help you deal with the stress, and hopefully help you relax.

2. When and How to Carve Out "Me Time"

Putting aside time for you can be a difficult thing to wrap your head around, but it is as important as scheduling a meeting with clients or making an appointment to go to the doctor. Making a special meeting or an appointment with yourself to do anything of your choosing can go a long way. It could be to relax in the bath or read a book for 30 minutes a day. If you don't have that much time, then start as small as you need. The point is to make this a priority. It is amazing how this can help you with stress and make you feel better about yourself.

I have learned how to meditate and although I may not be very good at it, I have developed some strategies to shut my brain off from the daily stressful activities. In the past I had trouble sleeping because I could not shut my brain off from reviewing things that happened in my day. My husband started to read to me and what I learned is that when I listen to novels my brain relaxes and finally, I am able to sleep. Now I listen to audio books.

Your activity is to find something that will help you relax and shut your brain off to what has gone on during your day. Don't be afraid to try multiple things. It may not be the first activity you choose, but when you find ways to relax your body and your mind, it is amazing how much more energized you will feel the next day. Be open to trying different strategies.

4

Values

I was taught to value life and enjoy every moment we have because you never know when your moments will be over. We are all going to leave this life at some point, it is the when and how that we don't know. This was one of the main reasons I wanted to write a book to help others navigate the issues we deal with, because life is too short to lose the person you want to become. During my many experiences, I have changed and developed along the way. For me, boredom will set in when I am not challenged. Thus I have to continue to move forward in my professional career in order to feel satisfied. This is why I tend to make different career moves every three or four years. I value growth and change; it keeps me motivated in my work and that is one of the reasons why the teaching profession works for me.

I also believe we have to respect our own values when helping others. Ask yourself if you can live with the fact that the people you are helping may not share your values. If the answer is yes, then just keep going with the job you have and you're most likely staying true to your personal values. If the answer is no, then you may want to reassess your values or realign them to fit with a different job or different work. As well, one note of caution: be careful not to push your values on someone else. This can be dangerous and could come back to haunt you because if a client's life goes awry after listening to you, then you are usually the first person they blame. This can be stressful for you and harmful for them.

We all change and grow and so may our values. These are individual ideas that make us who we are. Don't compromise who you are for the sake of an organization. In this chapter we will explore how to choose the right job for you and how this vocation can fit into your value system. At the end of the chapter, you will complete some activities that will help you identify your values and stay true to yourself in your professional choices.

Losing Yourself

The demands of our helping jobs sometimes require us to put in a little extra of ourselves, but if we are careful not to lose ourselves in our work, we should be able to stay grounded and focused on the personal things we value the most. If you are not able to do this then maybe it is time to look for a change and adjust your priorities (as I will discuss in the next chapter).

Sometimes I take the opportunity to reflect on who I was before and after I had children. Before I had children, my focus was on developing my skills as a teacher. I used to spend hours every day making sure my assignments were prepped and marked. I would volunteer to do many activities within the school and on the weekends, I would spend time with my friends. After I had children, my priorities changed. I did not have as much time to devote to extra-curricular activities at school and I rarely went out with friends. Any spare time I had would be devoted to my children and making sure I spent as much time as I could with them. My priorities had changed.

It is hard to pinpoint what our values are when our priorities are constantly changing; the activity at the end of the chapter may help make yours clearer. As well, we need to remember and accept that values may change over time. What you valued ten or twenty years ago may be different than what you value today. We grow up with the values our parents had and then we adapt them into our own value system at some point. We are always evolving as human beings and so, too, our value systems will continue evolving. You may want to revisit your values or discuss them with a partner. Either way, continue to look at them and work at understanding what is important to you as a person.

Values—Every Person Is Unique

Values can be a very tricky topic because everyone has a different opinion and we have to learn to respect and accept other people's values. Your philosophy on helping other people is hopefully in line with why you became a Helper in the first place. We can get lost in, "I have to have a job," but if the job is taking over your life or not allowing you to be yourself, then maybe it is time for a new job. I am not saying everyone should go out and quit their current job because it doesn't align with their values. I am saying that maybe it is time for a different job or a lateral transfer to a new job within the organization. In tough financial times this can be difficult, but perhaps doing something in your personal life that fulfills your need to help may be what needs to happen while searching for that ultimate job. Don't beat yourself up because you need to have an income to live!

I am very fortunate there is a wide range of jobs within the teaching profession. For example, if I want to teach a subject I am passionate about in a large classroom of thirty students, the opportunity is there. If I want to work with behaviour students or special education or become a district helping teacher, those types of jobs do come available. All of these unique jobs can bring variety to a vocation and they can help breathe new life into a career if people want a change. Before considering leaving your current organization, it might be worth a discussion with your manager or boss about changing your role from within. Right now you would have nothing to lose; one never knows what may come out of a simple conversation.

Pay is another issue. Changing jobs could mean a reduction in pay, and let's face it, the helping professions are usually at the lower end of the pay scale to begin with, which I don't understand. We are out there working with people to try to better their lives or help them through some terrible situations that can be hard for us to compre-hend, and we are not working for very much money. It seems a little backwards to me. It is sad that Helpers are working very hard with little financial reward, and people are only in these careers because they want to help people.

But if being a Helper makes you feel fulfilled—as it does for me—then maybe the pay doesn't matter in the end. There is no replacement for the natural reward we get from watching someone come from a disheartening situation to a good place.

Support for Finding a New Job

If money is a priority for you, then you need to make sure you find a profession that will pay you what you are worth. There *are* ways to make money with what we do. There are many job "head-hunters" out there that can help. Sometimes outsiders can give you some great insights and ideas you may not have thought of. For example, I knew a woman who had many skills and was quite capable of being in management but when her company downsized, she lost her job. After a year of trying to find a great job that suited her personality on her own, she did not find anything and was losing sight of what she wanted. She decided to go to an employment agency that helped her look at what type of employment would suit her values. She is now working at a job she loves, with a firm that really takes care of her and she is so happy when she talks about what she does, she is burst-ing with pride and enthusiasm. It is amazing, and rewarding, when you find your niche. Follow your instincts and your inner voice—it is worth listening to.

How to Choose the Right Job for You

Change can be very scary for anyone, but if you are staying true to your values, you will continue to feel good about yourself. Happiness is rarely bought, it is created. By maintaining integrity between your values and your professional life, you can also find the freedom to start creating happiness in your personal life if you have not already done so. Happiness can just spill over into all aspects of your life if you let it and are open to it.

Finding activities to help develop your life on a "soul" level can also help you to focus on the vocational choices that are true to your value system. Dr. Bernie Siegel discusses this concept in his workbook *101 Exercises for the Soul; A Divine Workout Plan for Body, Mind, and Spirit.*

> Everyone needs to answer for themselves what they are here to do. What are you looking for? What will allow you to feel at peace when you achieve your destination? What are you here to accomplish and do in your lifetime to give it meaning?[14]

There are a lot of activities in Siegel's book to help you focus on staying true to who you are. We are all striving to find the vocation that will keep us motivated and fulfilled with the work we do. And guess what? It is ok not to know what you would like to do next; this is why we refer to life as a "journey". You are eventually going to find what you are looking for and all the lessons you learn along the way will become a part of the growth you embrace.

Is Your Time Valuable?

How many hours do you put in at work? It may seem that you can always do more and your job may still never get done. And this may be true, especially when you work in an area where there is a constant need for making notes and doing paperwork. Paperwork is often a very important part of the profession; it can seem endless. There are always times when you could put more hours in and do more work to catch up. However, when do you draw the line?

I have often felt overwhelmed. I use the analogy of swimming underwater: I can see the surface, but no matter how hard I try to get to the top for air I cannot make it. This is what being overwhelmed feels like to me. What does it feel like for you?

So how do we manage these feelings and deal with the crazy demands of our jobs? How do we make our jobs fit into our lives instead of trying to fit our lives into our jobs? This is a question I have grappled with throughout my career.

It is important to strike the balance I talked about in the last chapter but it is also important to keep your integrity intact. Follow your values and value yourself. You need to make sure you take care of yourself because no one else is going to do that for you. In the last chapter we talked about how to keep your body healthy and how to keep your mind healthy. Now we are talking about how to keep your energy level or your spirit healthy.

Looking in the mirror every day and telling yourself that you did the best job you could do with the skills you have, is one healthy strategy. Watching someone do better in their lives because they met you is also a rewarding way to keep your soul healthy. Hold on to those moments and never let them go because they are true gifts (more about gifts in Chapter 10). They help to keep our values intact and our entire being healthy.

How do you do this? You need to make sure you are not losing yourself at work. You need to set some boundaries and do your best to stick to them. Without boundaries, companies, other people, even well-meaning family and friends may inadvertently take advantage of you. The worst thing about being a Helper is that we are so willing to help that we tend to forget to say no.

. . .

Points to Remember

- Ask yourself—does your vocational choice fall within your value system?
    - If not, can you live with that long term and still keep yourself emotionally healthy and charged?

- Try not to lose yourself in the work
    - This is dangerous to mind, body and soul

- Everyone is unique and so is your value system

- Make sure you fill your time with meaningful work and personal fulfillment

Chapter 4 Challenge & Activity

1. Understanding What is Important to You

If you had to go live on a deserted island and you could only take 10 things you find important, what or who (you can include people) would you want to take? After making your list, rank them from 1 to 10—1 being the most important and 10 being the least. Once they are ranked, take away five items you believe you could live without. This is a way to check that you have ranked them accordingly because if you are not taking away the bottom five then they are incorrectly ranked. Now you have a list of the five things you value the most.

This type of activity is interesting to do with your significant other. Once you have ranked your 10 most valued items get your partner to rank theirs and compare. After discussion about what each person would find important, both people need to narrow the items down to five. As a couple, try to agree together what your top five would be. Were your original lists the same or different? This can spark some great couple discussions.

Another variation would be to do this with a small group of friends. The best strategy for a small group is to do a "think, pair, share". That is, first you think about the activity and individually rank your 10 items. Then in pairs do the same but each person has to agree with the list. Finally, in small groups of four complete a list of 10 where each person has to agree on the order and item. The discussions that come from this activity can be amazing.

When I have done this activity with both youth and adults, they tend to value similar things; it is when you go beyond the top two where topics can vary greatly. Another variation would be to give a list of 10 valuable things and have a variety of people or a group of friends rank them. Youth may need a little more guidance along the way to help keep the activity moving. Make sure there is a debrief session at the end so that all questions are answered and observations are made. This debrief can help you gain insight into how people feel about themselves and their friends.

Family can be a little trickier because there are a lot of emotions invested within family dynamics. Plus your family is usually raised with the same values passed on from the parents and if you deviate there could be trouble within. Family members may be offended if you don't value what they value. Once again, it could spark some great conversation; however, take care to be respectful of others during the discussions. Raw emotions can come out and you want to make sure everyone feels good after the activity.

See Appendix F for two templates and suggested variations of this challenge.

2. Staying True to Your Values

Now that you have been able to focus on the values you have, you can take this to the next level. Ask yourself these simple questions:

1. Are you being true to your values both personally and professionally?
2. Does your work fit in with the values you have?
3. Can you live with other people in your life who may not have the same values? Work with them? Have them as clients?

If you have answered "no" to any of the above questions, then you may want to look into making a change. You need to make sure that at the end of the day you can look yourself in the mirror and be happy with who you have become. If this is not the case, then maybe it is time for a switch or to take a break from what is currently going on in your life. We as Helpers have to be careful we are not going down a road that is uncomfortable and does not feel right. We have gut instincts or an inner voice for a reason and when we don't listen, that is when our own lives feel unstable or we don't feel harmonious within ourselves.

A good resource is *What is Holding You Back? Thirty Days to Having the Courage and Confidence to Do What You Want, Meet Whom You Want, and Go Where You Want*, by Sam Horn.[15] She has a month-long process that helps you feel more confident and able to move forward with the life that will meet your needs and values. It is worth a look.

5

Developing Boundaries with
Patience and Flexibility

In this chapter we explore boundaries, in depth. We'll look at why we need them, how we can achieve them, and how we can set them with clients. Maintaining personal boundaries is key to taking care of yourself. Looking back, many of the times things were not working very well for me, I did not have clear boundaries or expectations of myself and others. For example, when I did not set boundaries at work, I had little time to spend with my family. At home, spending all my time with family left me little time for exercise. We all have pressures that can creep into our worlds and we need to be aware of them and make sure we set ourselves up for success by standing our ground, no matter how difficult it may become. Jan Black and Greg Enns sum it up best in their book, *Better Boundaries; Owning and Treasuring Your Life*,

> When you are clear on where you end and others begin, when you adopt full ownership of your life, and when you're your own best friend, you will naturally build better boundaries and therefore a finer, more caring life.[16]

Your personal boundaries are tested every day, so are you prepared to enforce these to stay true to who you are? We will explore how you have to live with some harsh realities in your work, how your reality is different from your clients', and how to communicate with clients when you are angry. We need to remember that our clients will be developing and growing on their own timeline—not ours. Helpers need to have the patience to allow clients to dictate how and when their own change(s) will come about.

Boundaries—Who Needs Them?

All youth go through a stage in their lives where life is only about them. They seem oblivious to their surroundings. Parents struggle through this time and usually feel like their children or teenagers are never going to grow up. I have labeled this era in a young person's life the *Me, Myself and I* syndrome. Even the nicest youth have a time when it is all about them.

"Mom, what are you going to make for dinner?"

"Mom, can you drive me to my friends because we have to work on a project that is due tomorrow and we need to use their computer."

"Mom, have you done the laundry because I am running out of clothes."

It doesn't matter that you have just gotten home from work and you have a report due the next day yourself. Nothing has been started for dinner and you need to do laundry because your weekend had been spent watching them play sports thus not doing your chores that needed to get done. As parents, we need to stand our ground, but at the same time respect the youth for who they are too.

Youth tend to have a hard time expressing thanks for the hours you put into their lives. One day, I had a particularly difficult time at work. Many students had made requests of me that I felt did not value my time at all and on top of that, the demands were for things I could not accomplish. After work, I went to pick up my children at our daycare provider's house. This woman is a saint, as far as I am concerned. She is a single mom with five of her own children. She cares for other people's young children (mostly under the age of five) all day while raising teenagers herself. She and I were talking about our respective days when her son came in and told her he needed to eat dinner soon because he had to go to work by 6:00 pm. It was about 5:30 pm at this time. He was complaining she needed to hurry up and make him dinner. I wondered what was wrong with him. I finally said to the daycare provider, "There seems to be a lot of *Me, Myself and I* going around."

She and I started laughing. Then we started talking about examples of how this was going around. Although it did not help the situation that she and I were both in, we did have a great laugh—a therapeutic laugh. If I can give anyone advice of how to survive working with and raising teenagers, it is to laugh often. Laugh at the different situations you face. Laugh at things you do that may not work. Life will be less stressful for everyone involved. I will talk about this at great length when I discuss laughter being the best medicine in Chapter 8.

I believe we need to set boundaries with our own children. When I am busy I feel guilty if I don't have the energy to uphold these boundaries. We have to understand life is not going to be perfect. We, as Helpers, are usually dealing with people who are struggling and feel out of control. This can and may happen to you in your personal life. Can you live with this?

We also have to understand there will be problems in life we cannot fix. To be effective Helpers, we have to acknowledge we are just guiding our clients or students along in their journey; it is their journey to take. As a human being you have to be able to live with the fact that sometimes you will not be able to change the horrible things these people are going through and this is something you need to live with.

To learn more about the *Me, Myself and I* syndrome, please see Appendix G.

Living with Reality

There are some situations that will be beyond your control. Another thing we have to be careful of is not to tell clients what to do based on our own agenda rather than theirs. Throughout my career I have come across some pretty awful events both personally and professionally and these situations have rocked me to the core; this is the stuff we cannot talk to our loved ones about because it is so hard to comprehend ourselves. As Helpers, we want to be like Superman and come in and save the day for them. But these are situations where we need to have acceptance of their agendas. The best help we can give our clients is to give them proper tools so they can make positive changes.

This reminds me of the old adage, you can lead a horse to water but you cannot make him drink. As Helpers, we can show clients or tell clients about shelters or helpful organizations, but if they are not ready to leave their terrible situations, we cannot force them to. This is their life.

However, this part is easier said than done. I have had many nights in my life where I have lost sleep because I have laid awake thinking of all the horrible things that may happen to the young adult I was working with. This is when I need to make sure I am taking care of myself. People who are not in the helping profession may not understand all of the horrible or ugly things we deal with in a week. These tough situations are hard for me to deal with—even given I am a trained professional.

Day in and day out, we are consistently trying to support people who are lacking the skills to do so. We need to be careful because there will come a time when things may be too much for us to deal with or we take on too many issues and we will suffer. These are the times we need to move clients on to another professional who is trained to deal with the issues that we cannot.

Also, there may be times when the issue is too big for you to deal with alone and you may need to have a consulting group to guide you along. Know when these issues are too much for you to personally deal with and seek assistance and support when necessary.

Beware of Other People's Reality

People are as unique as the vocations they work in and each of us—no matter our chosen field—has to deal with different types of issues and stressors. What we, as Helpers, have to deal with may be difficult to navigate for someone working in a different field. Be aware that some of what you do may be difficult for other people to comprehend.

One day, I was talking to my brother. We were going to a community charity event together and we had not really seen much of each other for a while, so we were catching up. My week at school had been pretty bad and I had found out about some horrible abuse that had happened to two different students. One bad story in a month is one thing but two bad situations with two different individuals this early in my career was another. My brother asked how I was doing and I started talking about how much abuse there seems to be in the world. I spoke generally because of confidentiality but even this was too much for him. He asked me to stop talking about these issues because they were horrible things to get in his head. I really respected him for this because he was clearly showing his boundaries and I don't blame him. Discussing tough situations and stories are things that should be done with people with the proper training. I also realized that if I, as a Helper, was having a difficult time dealing with these issues how could I expect my brother—with no training in this field—to deal with them?

There are some boundaries you need to uphold. Young people need boundaries and we are pretty good at setting them up for our own children, but what about us? We need to set them too. There are times when we need a break or we need to use the word "no" more often than we do. When we are pushed into things we did not want to do in the first place, we can become bitter and upset with other people. We need to own what we can and recognize what we cannot do.

So how do we set boundaries? Developing and understanding boundaries is a very complex activity. The good news is, once you focus in on them and set them as your priority, you will be happy with who you become. Jan Black and Greg Enns discuss how to name and discover your personal statements which help to discover who you are and how you want to live your life:

> Your existing boundaries are a result of what you think about yourself.... Becoming aware of your sense of self-worth will help you to recognize what types of personal boundaries you need to develop.
>
> The best motive for setting boundaries is simply to value yourself enough to *protect* yourself from harm, *preserve* yourself for fulfillment, and *present* yourself for service. This is the essence of befriending yourself, and it requires an ongoing awareness of what beliefs are influencing your choices.[17]

Their work has ramifications for everyone because they break down the essence of why we need boundaries, and they present ideas on how we can achieve the ultimate life we strive for. Black and Enns also encourage readers to forgive ourselves for mistakes we may make along the way. They consistently remind us no one is perfect, but we have an opportunity to learn from our mistakes and consequently develop better boundaries in the future.

Where to Start?

We have to learn to prioritize our activities and decide what we can accomplish now, and what should be put off for another day. One possible way is using the "to do list" method. I am the type of person that has a multitude of "to do lists" for both work and home. It is funny how my life really has become a list. This is partly because I have become pretty forgetful and I am scared I will miss something if I don't write it down to remind myself. What is good about having it written down is I can look at what tasks need to be done now and which ones I can do later on in the week or delegate to someone else.

This can be a little trickier to do at work, especially if you are the only one doing a specific job. As Helpers, we have to realize we may not get to everything on our desk or to all the paperwork we have to complete. We will get to it, but we may not meet every deadline that has been set. There are some projects or reports that may take precedence and those are the ones we need to complete first, but there are many days where I know I am not going to get some of my work done on time and I, along with my supervisor, deal with this. A possible way to work this out is to make sure you build extra time in for each project you do at work so the pressure is off.

We have to take care of ourselves and we may want to consider making a change if we are having a difficult time setting boundaries at work. Helpers have one of the highest burnout rates because we usually end up doing more work for less pay. When cuts happen, they just get two people to do the work of four. I have talked to social workers where it is not uncommon for them to have 125 active files they are working on. How can we, as a society, expect a perfect job to be done when this is common practice? As in all helping professions, we need to take responsibility to take care of ourselves.

What to Do When Life Becomes Overwhelming

There can be times in your job when life is too overwhelming and the work starts to get to you. You, as a helping professional, need to listen. Observe your clients and yourself—are you being effective? You are the expert on you, and only you can answer this question. Be honest with yourself.

When your body needs some rest, then maybe you need to take a sick day. Only you will be able to understand when you need a break or change. You need to pay attention to the signs and follow your heart and head to make positive decisions and choices for yourself. Someone once told me that a change can be as good as a break. Leaving a job can be very difficult but if this is the best situation for you, then you need to take it and not be scared of change.

It is not just in your work life that you need to learn to say no, you have to learn how to do this with your family and friends as well. I have a large family and we all live close to one another but there are times when I cannot attend every family function. We are always trying to figure out the best way to spend our time and when you don't have very much time to give, it is even more important to make sure you stick to your boundaries. Family and friends will understand if you cannot go to every function, but you need to make sure you are not missing them all. I am not saying we should ditch every birthday party or family gathering, but if you have to miss a function once in a while, don't beat yourself up. It is not very relaxing when you get pulled in so many different directions.

In the book, *The Disease to Please*, Harriet Braiker discusses the people pleasing syndrome and if you have it, she gives some methods of how to avoid the pitfalls many people run into. There is a chapter dedicated to the concept of how we say "yes" when we really mean "no". We, as Helpers, need to give ourselves permission to say "no". By setting this boundary you are not a bad person, you are a smart person!

There are times when you may have done things for others even when you didn't want to, but that should not occur every time they ask; it should be those times when your friend or family member needs your help. The book goes on to discuss how this can feel like talking in a foreign language.[18] That is why the challenge at the end of this chapter is practicing the skill of saying "no".

Don't Communicate with Clients When You're Angry

Another important boundary to talk about is to avoid discussions when you are angry. Although we have discussed this earlier with examples of colleagues, it is worth mentioning again, especially in reference to talking to clients or young people. Waiting to have a discussion when we are calm is easier said than done, especially when it comes to family. When I discipline my children or we get into an argument, sometimes I find it quite difficult to walk away because there is no way I am letting a ten year-old tell me what to do.

When it comes to clients, it is doubly important to resist discussion when you are angry. I learned this very quickly in my first year of teaching a very needy and unique population of students. One of the young ladies in my English class had a developmental disability. We were having a group discussion and she was upset because I would not spend extra time with her that day, so she decided she would take a match and try to light her t-shirt on fire to catch my attention. When I was working the room helping everyone individually, I smelled smoke and asked if anyone knew where it was coming from. After about a minute I saw the fresh burn holes in her shirt and the book of matches she had in her hand. I was beyond shocked. There is no manual in our teacher training to suggest how I would deal with this.

I took away the matches and asked her to stay after class. In my head I was thinking what if she had successfully lit her shirt on fire? What would I have done? I was so upset about the risk she had taken with herself and the other students. I did not want to say anything I would regret, plus I knew I had to tell the appropriate administration immediately, and arrange for a counsellor to come in and support me with this student.

When I saw her after class I was still so angry and scared of the "what if" scenarios that I did not know what I was going to say. She kept apologizing and while I acknowledged her apology, I told her I was too upset to talk to her about it right now and we would discuss it the next day.

If I had spoken to her when I was angry there could have been horrible consequences. Words can really hurt, especially when working with students who have intellectual disabilities because they don't always understand or have the skills to navigate the complexity of emotions. I do know when I spoke to this student the next day, she understood the seriousness of the situation, and in the end this result was better than a lecture would have been.

Being, and Taking Care of, Yourself

It is good in our profession to be a human being and not try to be someone that you are not. It is ok to let your client know you are not having a good day. If you are honest with people that you are not feeling good or that you did not get much sleep, the session may go a little more smoothly for everyone involved. When we, as Helpers, try to be our clients' friends or our children's friends, things can get complicated very quickly. We have to be ourselves and care for these people, but there are boundaries to these relationships. Going out for coffee with a client to discuss their issues or hold a session in a different space for a change is fine, but going out with clients on a personal level is not fine. Letting clients call you at all hours of the day just lets them continue to take from you and you are never able to shut work off.

Proper rest for our bodies is essential, and when we are not getting the appropriate amount of rest we suffer and usually our health suffers. If you work until you are ready to drop then who will be there to pick up the pieces? You will end up taking more time off in the long run because you wore yourself out. When you need some rest, it is not time to be a martyr and show up at work. We are not doing anyone a favour coming to work sick, and it is self-centered for us to assume no one can replace us.

Can You Live with Uncertainty?

Another area of the helping profession that we need to have boundaries with, or understanding of, is the large world of uncertainty all around us. Many people don't like that there is no right way or wrong way. There is no manual that will work for everyone, and as a professional, understanding this is your first step to great success. That said, there are definitely many books to help guide you through support and suggestions but at the end of the day, if you don't learn to have patience and be flexible, you will not work as well with your clients and usually you will personally suffer.

Life is full of uncertainty. We cannot predict when our children or significant other will get sick. Where does patience come from when there are things going on in our personal lives that we cannot control? I don't have all the answers, but what I do know is we need to make sure our lives are in relatively positive working order to be able to help other people navigate their own.

If you cannot park your personal life at the door when you walk through it every morning then you will not be able to help your clients. If this continually becomes a problem for you, maybe it is time to take a break or time off or even try to find a new job in a similar or even completely different field. There are many interesting opportunities in our communities and sometimes it is amazing how we can improve things with a little change.

Whose Agenda Are You Dealing With?

When you project your own values or agenda on your clients, you don't let them make their own choices. In that case they will not have a positive response to working with you. Is that really helping? I worked with young adults on making career choices throughout their later high school years. A few times I had placed students out as a volunteer within companies I knew. Things fell apart quickly if the student really did not want to be there. I had not listened to what they wanted. I just wanted them to go and gain some work experience because I thought I knew what they needed and so I pushed this on them. If there is anything I have learned it is that we need to let our clients drive the agenda.

If you start telling the client what is in their best interest, then you are using your own agenda and you are trying to change who your clients are and how they should be in this world. You need to respect them and be flexible enough to let them change when they are ready. No two days in anyone's life will be the same and no two days with your clients will be the same. If you can live with having the client in the driver's seat, than you will be a better Helper in the end.

You need to make sure you can stay in the helping profession long term. Job markets are unpredictable, but people will continue to need support. If, as a Helper, you can feel good about yourself personally and spend time enjoying yourself and your friends, then you will be able to balance this difficult job and a personal life.

. . .

Points to Remember

- Need to set boundaries:
    - personally
    - professionally
    - with clients

- Boundaries work two ways

- Example of a boundary: Don't communicate with clients when you are angry

- Learn to live with harsh realities
    - Don't dump your emotional baggage on others—crosses into their personal boundaries
    - Your reality may be different than other people's reality—respect that

- Remember to have patience and flexibility
    - Let clients dictate their own growth
    - Helpers need to live with the client's timeline not dictate one

Chapter 5 Challenge & Activity

1. How to Use the Word "No"

One of the biggest challenges we have in life is saying no to people. Helpers are especially bad at this! We tend to agree with helping people out because we have this immense need to give to others.

Your challenge is to think of something you really don't want to do but have agreed to do in the past. Then practice on your own with a response using the word "no" in a kind but firm way. Practice your facial expressions in the mirror. Next, think of what the other person or group's response will be and prepare some answers. Then run through the entire exercise again from the beginning. You will be amazed how people respond when you have anticipated their responses and have an answer.

2. Setting Boundaries

Think of 20 activities you have done in the past month. Write each activity in the appropriate columns based on whether or not the activities are in your best interest. For example:

Column A	Column B
Activities that **were** in my best interest	Activities that **were not** in my best interest

Next, decide what boundary areas they were breaking—personal, work or professional. Label each boundary in the columns. After reviewing the data, pick one or two of the boundaries you would like to try to work on in the next month with the goal of improving your abilities to set better boundaries.

Some examples are when you have had a long week at work and you don't want to go out with a group of friends, but they are pressuring you to do so. A response to this situation could be, "Thanks for making sure I am included, but I am going to relax at home tonight. Can we schedule some time next week instead? Are you free this Friday?"

This will give you the opportunity to make sure your friends do not feel ignored and that you have the chance to do what you want the day you were supposed to go out with them. Practicing how you would like to respond to your friends' comments (especially if they have made you feel guilty in the past), will help you when you are trying to assert your personal boundaries. Trying out a script in your head beforehand may help with your responses as well.

Another aspect of this activity is giving yourself praise for those times when you are asserting your personal boundaries to protect the aspects of your life that are priorities. Review the activities you listed in Column A and congratulate yourself for your ability to align your needs with your actions. Hopefully there will be an increasing number of activities in Column A as time goes by when you are staying true to yourself.

See Appendix H for the worksheet that corresponds to this activity.

6

Challenges Helpers Face

How do we, as Helpers, make sense of a world that, at times, doesn't make sense? I grapple with this on a daily basis. My team consistently deals with issues that are so large we begin to wonder if it is possible to make a positive change on the issue, let alone feel we have a positive effect on the world. There are days when I come home after a tough day thinking I might as well quit for the amount of good I've done. These are the days it is most important to hang onto your own sense of self-worth.

At the *Power Within* seminar, Anthony Robbins,[19] the keynote speaker, said something that resonated with me: he asked if we had ever noticed that "common sense is not so common." Yes, I have noticed this! There have been times where I think I am on another planet when talking to people. I have found when I talk about my career with someone who does not work as a Helper, they tend to either think that I am too harsh or that I need to be stricter (or both!). It is amazing how people can be so opinionated about something they have not dealt with before. A lot of people act like they know what they are talking about, but their ideas don't seem to be based in common sense. Working with people or dealing with the public, it is all about having common sense and at times, I feel there are so many people who don't have it or use it.

In this chapter, we explore challenges we face as Helpers. We encounter many challenges in our jobs, such as the challenge to accept the things that are beyond our control, to understand that change is difficult and takes time, to have flexibility to roll with what is happening, and to learn from our own mistakes. We also have to accept that we don't have all the answers and there are many resources available to help us through difficult situations.

Accept What Is Beyond Your Control

As a Helper, accepting what is beyond our control can be challenging. It is ingrained in us that we need to help, but then as a Helper we can be tempted to overstep the fine line and go beyond our scope, which can be both dangerous and unhelpful. If we infuse ourselves into other people's lives, then their problems have just become our problems. We have to try to detach ourselves from this way of thinking and helping. Setting boundaries or limits with others has to happen in order to help clients come up with their own solutions.

Once, after I had taken a course on mediation, I made the mistake of getting between parents and a youth to try to mediate home concerns. At the time, I thought I was helping this family navigate some pretty messy situations (hindsight is always 20/20!). I spent a lot of extra time trying to help out the family and they were continually calling and asking for more help from me to solve issues that had nothing to do with this student's education. I was so involved that I had crossed the line between helping and interfering.

It is very important that we understand our limitations and stay within them. I should have sent this family to another professional to deal with these separate issues. The lesson here is to understand when an issue has gone beyond your scope and contact someone who deals with those types of issues to work with the person or family. This issue also affected me mentally; it was draining me heavily to continue working at this level with this particular family, and it also took energy away from doing my job. Our jobs are hard enough without over-stepping our bounds and getting involved where we are not experts to deal with issues.

Change Is Difficult

People have to want to change themselves. We cannot do the changing for them. No matter how much we would like to see a change happen, it won't if they are not ready. Over the years I have worked with a lot of angry clients, both teenagers and adults. One of them once told me in some very choice words that I was not going to ever get him to do what I wanted him to do. I had obviously pushed him too far. Sometimes during discussions, we need to take a step back and let clients tell us when they are ready to move forward. David Burns states through his book, *Ten Days to Self-Esteem,* that it is important to let clients come forward on their own timeline and not yours.[20]

Some days clients will not make progress. Have the flexibility and wherewithal to know that discussing issues may not work that day; this acknowledgment will get you further ahead as a Helper than trying to impose your own agenda.

This does not mean you are a lousy Helper, it means that by listening and respecting your client in that moment, you are being a better Helper. Plus helping should always be about moving the client forward when they are ready and if they are not, we have to be prepared to accept that.

Keep in mind that working to change how a client thinks, acts or feels is a complicated process. As a Helper, you need to embrace the small steps that are made because the overall picture for the client can be very overwhelming for them. Personally our old habits are easier to use because one way or another this behaviour or habit is working for us.

When we try to introduce change within ourselves, we often find it a difficult process. This will be no different for our clients. Knowing this will help you have the patience you need to continue to work with a client that might not be moving forward as much as they need to. Change takes time because it is a difficult thing to do and comprehend.

Can We Be Impartial?

Sometimes it is also a challenge to have empathy and patience with people who have been through tough situations. We have to remember not to judge people because we don't know what it is like to live their life. All people deserve respect. It is easy for us to ask, why don't they go get a job, or why don't they look at how they could fix their problems instead of coming to us, but in reality they most likely have not been given the tools to do so. If we look at the problems society faces, most of the time they are systemic. Societal issues that families face are usually similar to what their parents faced. Thus the lessons they have been taught are passed on. If parents have not been given the tools to cope themselves with life, how in the world are they going to teach their children?

Take ten minutes right now and try some deep breathing to relax. Now visualize what your life would be like if you lost your job. Then think about how hard it would be to not have the funds to pay your bills or to provide for your family. What we can forget is sometimes we are just a few paycheques away from not being able to afford where we live. This is a great technique when you feel like you are starting to become judgmental or don't understand what one of your clients is going through. Spend some time thinking about how difficult their lives are. By trying to walk a mile in their shoes, you may have more patience with them in the long run.

My family is a pretty tight unit. We live close to one another and support each other anytime things may not be going well. Yes, there are days when I may not agree with every decision that is made in the family or I don't want them judging me for decisions I may make, but in the long run, their support is there.

If you have grown up surrounded with a supportive group of people, imagine what life would be like if they suddenly disappeared. How would you cope? Where would you go for help? The next time someone walks into your office, think about what your life would have been like if you had gone through all that these people have had to go through. I don't believe anyone wakes up in their life and says I want to end up homeless and on welfare all my life. Or I want to spend my life depressed or angry.

Things That Don't Make Sense

Another challenge I have found working in helping professions has been trying to make sense out of horrific things. How can I go home and live a normal life when the youth I am working with are on the streets or maybe they are spending the night in custody of the police? It can be very difficult to separate and shut out all the negative aspects of a job and not let them spill over into our personal life. What can we as Helpers do? The simple answer is not to let it become part of your personal life, but the reality is this is easier said than done.

This is when we need to find ways to release these feelings. This can be done by exercise, therapy, or relaxation techniques. This is individual so you need to find what works for you to get through the tough days. Knowing yourself and what your limits are is an important part of making sure you are okay. Seek professional support when needed. I have expanded on both of these topics in different chapters but it is important to repeat it here. You need to take care of yourself and make sure you are processing the information that is coming your way in a healthy manner just as much as trying to take care of your client.

Other People's Failures—How Do We Deal With Them?

It is very challenging letting other people fail and learn. As a Helper you want to come in and save the day. I had to really discover the value of sitting back and letting youth fail because if I didn't, they would never learn from their mistakes and, let's face it, we all learn the same way. This is where experience comes into play. We have to learn from the mistakes we make and build up the strength to move on. I have always told my students that it is not making the mistake that makes you a good person; it is what you do after the mistake.

I had a student who learned how to drive on a farm at an early age and was allowed to work the machines for his family to earn some extra funds on the weekends. He was able to drive very well and thought it would be no big deal to drive a car before he got his driver's license. He was not even sixteen years old yet.

One Saturday night he took his parents' car without permission and drove his friends around. Unfortunately, in the bad weather he did not see an elderly gentleman crossing the road. The youth swerved to miss him and skidded the car into a tree. Both passengers and driver suffered life-threatening injuries. Fortunately, everyone survived. The youth, however, is still dealing with the consequences of his actions today. He will not be allowed to get a driver's license for a long time and he does not even want to work with the farm equipment anymore. He has difficulties getting into a car. The consequences of these split-second decisions have had a lasting impact on all those involved.

Now that this incident is over, what does the youth do next?

Consequences after Mistakes

This is an extreme example to use, but it definitely illustrates on a large scale how mistakes can spiral out of control quickly before you realize it. Things can start off as innocent thoughts and then become large mistakes you can't take back. A possible outcome of this situation could have been for the young men that were in the car to discuss how one little decision changed all of their lives that night. It is easy for us to sit back and throw the book at people or give our opinion when they mess up, but we sure don't look at what we need to do afterwards or how to help people through the emotional turmoil after. We have to live with our consequences—are you going to hide in a closet or move on with your life? Many people live with severe guilt, and need some supports with how life can go on after their mistakes have been made so their life won't spiral out of control.

Guilt can eat a person alive. Joan Borysenko describes it best in *Guilt is the Teacher, Love is the Lesson*, "Mistakes were an open invitation to self-criticism, anxiety, depression, paranoia, and even panic."[21] She suggests we need to be careful to not fall into the vicious cycle of guilt. There are so many issues that can stem from this cycle:

> Worse still, I was angry much of the time (and nice people shouldn't be angry right?). Unable to forgive myself or anyone else, I was a prisoner of guilt and resentment. I did my best to hide all this underneath a smile but was ultimately betrayed by my body, which became a breeding ground for stress-related illnesses ranging from high blood pressure and migraine headaches to a spastic colon and constant respiratory infections.[22]

If we focus on feeling guilty over every mistake we make, we will lead ourselves down an unhealthy path. This will have consequences with our health and welfare. These are traps we have to make sure we don't fall into as Helpers.

Thus when youth and adults make mistakes, we need to help support them in making it right, without giving them our own value systems. How do we do this? When people are lacking skills, we need to teach them the skill set in order for them to address their problems and learn what to do after they make mistakes. I call this the skill set "tool box". A builder cannot go onto a job site without taking his tools to build with. This is the same for people learning social, life and emotional skills. Clients need to learn skills (tools) and how to use them. This is where the Helpers come in (See Appendix I for some resources on skill building).

As Helpers, we may understand a lot of what they are going through because we have had adversity in our lives, but we are not the same people and clients will react differently. Not everyone is the same. You cannot think for one minute that because you have had similar issues that you fully understand what others are going through. You really can only understand yourself.

Flexibility

As previously stated, when working with people, we need to be flexible. When teaching a group of people, you have the flexibility to adapt the lesson based on what they need in that moment. The best planned sessions sometimes will change as you go. Clients can be the same. You can predict what you think they might have issues with, but in the end, things are going to happen in the moment that you did not see coming. As well, when clients transition, it is important to try to think of everything that may go wrong. If you think of what you will do in each case, then you are as prepared as you can be. However sometimes, things will happen that you never thought of. This is okay, because you can make a note of how the issue was solved. Use these notes to learn and try new strategies the next time this issue arises; this way you learn from your mistakes and try not to repeat them.

We also need to remember that outlining the same consequences for all of our clients will not be effective for two reasons—we are there to guide and help, not tell them what to do, and this is projecting our values and experiences. Life is not black and white and thus our support should be open to all possibilities. We need to remind ourselves every day that helping is about other people and not us.

You Will Make Mistakes

Another thing to remember is that as a professional you are going to make mistakes too. What should you do when this happens? You have to be honest and take responsibility no matter the consequences of your actions.

I will never forget the time I had a new principal start with our program and of course within a week of them starting we had an incident where the police were called. What an introduction to our program! So this person, who does not know us or our program, now has to deal with a police incident where one of our students was fully in the wrong. I told her the facts of the situation. Her response was, what did you learn from this? I thought that was interesting; it was the first time I had not had to go into lots of details about who was at fault and give a myriad of details, which in the end did not matter. How innovative! I went through what I had been working out with our group in the debrief and the alternatives we had come up with. In the end, the meeting was to make sure we tried to avoid this type of incident in the future, and did not devolve to pointing fingers. We were able to focus on prevention instead of blame.

You will make mistakes both professionally and personally. What you should take away from a mistake are the life lessons learned and not the bad that may have occurred. Youth tend to blame everyone around them when they make mistakes. This is a common tendency for youth, and hopefully they grow out of this as part of the maturity process. This can be one factor for youth who continually seem to get themselves into trouble.

As adults, we need to learn to pick and choose our battles. When working on a goal behavior or some type of change, you want to make sure you focus on the specific behavior and let the minor stuff go. You need to pick and choose your battles because you are not able to work on everything all at once. It would be overwhelming for everyone involved.

The Helping Profession Is a Challenge

Helping professions in general are very challenging. We often feel like we understand what other people are going through but there is a big difference between empathy and knowing. One can only understand what we as individuals have gone through in our lives and not what other people have. It is important to be careful to not fall into the traps that other people place. Know your limitations and what your role is, and stick to those parameters. This will prevent you from falling into the trap of over-stepping or helping people you are not equipped to service.

As a child I read the Anne of Green Gables series. I love the line where Anne states "… tomorrow is a new day with no mistakes in it yet…"[23] I like this quote because after I make a mistake, I may feel very negative but if I take this to heart (that tomorrow will give us a fresh start), then I have something to look forward to.

Another mantra I like to live by is the Alcoholics Anonymous saying, "Take life one day at a time."[24] We need to remember we are people trying to help others and we will not be perfect.

There are some really good books with great suggestions on how to help your clients or students develop skills. These may help you bring new ideas to your individual or group sessions.

The Explosive Child, by Ross Greene

Better Boundaries; Owning and Treasuring Your Life, by Jan Black and Greg Enns

Embracing Uncertainty, by Susan Jeffers

Fighting Invisible Tigers, by Earl Hipp

Ten Days to Self Esteem, by David Burns

Feeling Good; The New Mood Therapy, by David Burns

The Unloading Zone—Anger Management Course, by Family Services of Greater Vancouver and author Catherine Hobson

There is not one set way to deal with issues—we have to learn by trial and error. Just remember tomorrow will bring a new day with no mistakes yet!

. . .

Points to Remember

- ‣ Accept what is beyond your control
  - – Be careful not to go from helping to interfering

- ‣ Change is difficult and it takes time
  - – Mistakes happen—help guide people through the healing of the mistake with both you and your clients
  - – When you make a mistake: focus on lessons to learn

- ‣ As Helpers, we need the flexibility to roll with what is happening

- ‣ Know what your role is with the clients
  - – Don't deviate
  - – Don't fall into the trap of thinking you know everything
  - – Reach out for resources and support

Chapter 6 Challenge & Activity

1. Detailing and Learning from Mistakes

The next time you make a mistake, write down the details. Then strategize ways it could have been prevented and what you can improve for next time. Keep track of these mistakes and "better solutions" for a month. After the month review the information to see if there is a pattern to your mistakes, and possibly your mindset or behavior. Be aware of possible triggers or ways that specific things may influence you to make more mistakes. Most importantly, forgive yourself and learn from your mistakes; this is how you grow as a person and this is what your clients need to do as well when they are ready.

This is a great activity to model with clients to teach them that everyone in the world makes mistakes; how we rectify these mistakes builds a strong foundation for a life of integrity. See Appendix J for a template for this challenge.

2. Improving Your Personal Tool Box

Teaching others how to improve their tool boxes of skills and responses when they make mistakes is an area my clients usually require the most work with. Before giving this activity to a client, I would suggest you try this yourself. It is easier to understand this exercise once you have attempted to do the same type of work.

A simple way to improve or help develop a tool box is to first figure out what a person is doing to get themselves into difficult situations. Thus the issues need to be broken down step-by-step or piece-by-piece. So the first step is to gather information from your client. Have them describe the last time they made a mistake and write all the information down. Ask them the following questions;

1. Were they happy with any of the outcomes?
2. Would they want the outcome to be different?

After going over this information with the client, figure out what skills they need to learn so the next time this situation comes up, the response will be different.

Here are some questions that may help:

1. Imagine what it would be like if you could magically have all your mistakes taken away—how would you feel?

2. What are some steps you need to take to make sure this mistake does not happen again, or is corrected if it does?

3. Are there any skills you need to learn to make sure this particular mistake does not happen again?

Author and behaviour expert Ross Greene talks about how no one wants to be "bad", people with behavioral issues may lack a certain skill-set to do well. If you teach them these skills then they will be able to perform at the appropriate level. It is a very interesting theory and one that may be useful for Helpers to explore.[25]

7

Knocking Out Negativity, Fear and Self-Doubt

I can do ten phenomenal things in my day, but when the day is over, I am tempted to look at the one thing I may have done wrong and analyze it to death. Why is that?

I believe we are, to a degree, hard-wired to focus on negativity instead of positivity. This happens a great deal in sport. If a team loses, there is a tendency to focus on everything the team did wrong.

We are all looking for positive results out of life and when they don't happen we tend to ask ourselves, why, or what did I do wrong, when in reality we can do everything right and life still may not work out the way we want it to.

If you can reframe how you look at events each day to be more positive, then your days will seem better and you will be happier. Focusing and building upon the positives instead of focusing on negatives can only help with your outlook on life. For example, in 2011 my house was broken into. My daughter was home alone when it happened and she hid from the intruders. They took our electronics, all of my jewelry and destroyed our front door. To add insult to injury, our insurance had lapsed and we did not end up renewing on time so there was no insurance coverage. Luckily, however, our daughter stayed safe!

Had my daughter not been at home I would have been so upset about the possessions I had lost. However, she was there, and I could not care less about not being able to replace my possessions. It was just stuff—my daughter is priceless! I stayed focused on that to help me through this troubling time.

As a Helper you need to continue to keep positive while working with clients as they can share some pretty heavy, awful information with you. You cannot let fear and self-doubt come into play with all aspects of your life. If you can continue to focus on the *"You can"* attitude you will be ahead in the long run.

You also need to remember that fear can be a paralyzing emotion which can prevent you from realizing your dreams. My father told me for years, you create your own realities in life and you are the only one who can control whether or not it will be positive or negative. Therefore, don't give in to the negativity around you and remember you deserve the good things that happen to you in your life.

Stomp Out Fear & Self Doubt

The problem with focusing on the negative is it can lead to fear and self- doubt. Self-doubt can paralyze us to the point where we are not able to move forward into any type of positive behaviour. For example, when things are going well in my life, I feel like I can do anything and conquer the world. When things are not going well, I am not happy and I tend to get negative with the way I act and talk. This is true for many people, so we need to remember to find a positive to focus on when things are not going well. We do our best work when we are feeling good about the rest of our lives.

Susan Jeffers, an author and speaker, refers to fear as a deterrent for people trying to focus on positive thoughts. During one of her workshops she presented the idea that if you only think positively your life would feel positive. She met a lot of resistance for this idea. People did not believe it was possible to always be positive. However when she asked her audience why, no one could give her an answer but they felt this was not very realistic. She told her audience the following:

It is reported that more than 90% of what we worry about never happens. That means that our negative worries have less than a 10% chance of being correct. If this is so, isn't being positive more realistic than being negative? Think about your own life. I'll wager that most of what you worry about never happens. So are you being realistic when you worry all the time? No!

If you think about it, the important issue is not which is more realistic, but rather, *"Why be miserable when you can be happy?"*[26]

These are important points because a lot of our fear comes from worrying too much about things that are beyond our control. If, as Susan Jeffers states, most of the things that worry us don't happen, then odds are what we fear will happen, won't.

Jeffers discusses how using positive words can help us avoid the fears we have and bring us to a place of happiness. If we continue to focus on our positive actions every day, even when we don't always believe them to be true, then we can become happier, more positive people. In her words, "Positive words make us physically strong; negative words make us physically weak. The amazing aspect of this experiment is that it doesn't matter if we *believe* the words or not. The mere uttering of them makes our inner self believe them."[27]

So the next time you feel what you are doing does not make a difference or you feel negative about things that are going on in your life, remember that speaking and thinking positively—even when you don't fully believe it—will change your outlook and attitude. Try doing the exercise at the end of this chapter—it will make a difference!

Using Self-Talk to Face Personal Fears

Everyone has fears. I have a fear of heights and at times I have been paralyzed to move forward due to this fear. We were in Mexico visiting the pyramids at Chichen Itza and I was climbing up the side of a pyramid. I was focusing on trying to get to the top to look around.

At one point, my husband told me not to look down because I was up quite high. So of course I looked down and then I was frozen. I did not feel comfortable going up or down. After fifteen minutes of trying to figure out what to do, I started to climb backwards in more of a crawling form to get myself down.

Since then, I have been put in a multitude of situations where heights are involved. I have slowly lessened my fear by using a technique called positive self-talk. For example, I tell myself the following;

> "I am going to be ok."
> "Nothing is going to hurt me."
> "I am safe."
> "I am not going to fall."
> "The building or structure is safe."
> "I can do this."

One day my trainer asked me what would happen if I did trust that people had secured the elevators and the high places within a stadium so that people don't fall. What would happen, he asked, if you could look out and enjoy a great view without anything happening? Right now, you are not enjoying any views but if you took just a small step towards that fear and just started chipping away at it then think about what you could gain.

He was right. Slowly, over time I have gotten better with heights. I am not perfect and I still tend to get nauseous, but I have been able to enjoy some beautiful views of the Grand Canyon, San Francisco and the St. Louis Arch as a result of using positive self-talk. Yes I still have times when I have to take a step back and regroup, but I have gained more than I have lost and now, when it comes to enjoying some awesome scenery I am willing to try new things instead of feeling paralyzed with fear. As Helpers, we can use positive self-talk with our clients or give the clients the exercises to try at the end of the chapter. It can make a difference with them too.

Self-Visualization Technique

Another form of changing negative thoughts to positive ones is through self-visualization. This technique works well with most people and is a good strategy you can use with your clients. It has helped many people I know overcome some big fears. So what is self-visualization? Basically you need to relax yourself and clear you mind of all things. Then imagine yourself doing something you are scared to do such as standing at the top of a high mountain, or giving a speech in front of a bunch of people. The key is to imagine a positive outcome. Visualizing yourself doing an activity with positive outcomes will help you be successful in addressing your fear.

I also teach meditation in combination with self-visualization. The deep breathing technique is very beneficial to everyone. In a class I was taking on counselling techniques the instructor stated that it can take a long time to perfect meditation and/or self-visualization, but the benefits of making your body breathe properly and deeply will help to clear your mind and give you focus. Don't be discouraged if either of these techniques does not work right away. There have been times when I have tried to teach the breathing techniques and people started to burst out loud laughing within a group. It is natural that we react nervously when pushing our boundaries, so if that happens, just keep working at it. (See Appendix K for suggestions and techniques for self-talk, self-visualization & meditation.)

Be careful to make sure your client is ready to learn new techniques. You can influence your clients to do what you want them to do but if you rush your client into something before they are ready, it can potentially have disastrous results. When in doubt about whether or not you are on the right track with your clients, survey your client and ask them directly if what you are doing is helping (Please see Appendix L for an example of a survey you could use).

How to React When It Feels Like Your Client Is Paralleling Your Reality

What should you do when a client comes in with negative thoughts that you have had to personally deal with in the past? This can happen and it is difficult for Helpers to deal with, because feelings from your past can surface quickly. Before you know it, the client is talking to you about something that seems very familiar. One of my professors once told me that feelings have no time. I truly believe this. That is why grief, sorrow, or being victimized can be so difficult to deal with because the emotions and feelings surrounding these issues can be close to the surface at any time.

Be careful to look at the situation in two ways: first, do you have the expertise to deal with this client? And second, is their issue something that is too close to your heart? Sometimes it is important, for us and them, to move them on to another person.

The feelings of grief and sorrow that come from loss lurk just below the surface every day of our lives. When we have reminders, we can become sad for the loss of these people, especially when they were close to us. These feelings of loss and grief can surface at any time. Feeling sad and dealing with these emotions later on in life is natural and normal. I truly believe this to be accurate.

As I mentioned earlier, some of my relatives were killed by a drunk driver in the fall of 1989. It was devastating for my family. This incident has changed my life and my thought process. For example, I have chosen to never to drink to excess. I do not ever want to feel out of control or make poor choices as a result of alcohol (the accident happened a month before my nineteenth birthday). It also taught me to enjoy every moment I have with my family and my children; enjoying the moments I have with my family are priceless. Sometimes we get so wrapped up with work, we forget to enjoy the little things.

At first, I was not ready to look at the more positive changes that happened as a result of this horrible incident. I did everything in my power to wreck relationships and I was a very negative person for a while. For years I was not myself.

Twenty-three years later, my girlfriend lost her five year-old to cancer and it brought up all these feelings again. They never left; they were just below the surface. The feelings I went through then were very raw and they tend to creep up when I least expected them to and they make me feel very sad. Again, this is normal behaviour and a very normal way to deal with the feelings surrounding a strained and stressful time.

As Helpers, we need to make sure we don't fall into the trap of giving our personal issues to the client. My suggestion is, when you feel an issue is too close to you, run what you are doing or the strategies you are using by a colleague or have a colleague sit through a session with you. The best way to make sure you are being objective is to ask a third party their opinion on what you are doing. This way everybody wins. It also does not make you a bad Helper to pass a client to someone else because the issues they are dealing with could possibly bring up hurtful and sad emotions for you. This does not make you weak, it makes you smart.

Fear = Paralyzing Emotion

Fear can be a paralyzing emotion. When we are fearful of moving on, we tend to get stuck where we are. Fear may crop up in our relationships with loved ones, in our families, with our health. Fear can bring life to a halt. Even the most put-together people let fear stand in their way at times.

Once, I was working with a particular youth who had difficulties with drugs and alcohol. I really wanted him to get some support but he felt trapped. The other adults around him would not help him move forward and he was so scared that he did not know what to do. The one stable relationship he felt he had was with his pet rat. He was scared to do anything about his addictions until he knew his rat would be taken care of. With a little guidance—and with my colleague's offer to take care of his pet rat—this boy was able to take the step forward to try to get himself some support for his addiction.

Sometimes as Helpers we really do go above and beyond. My

colleague offering to take care of the rat was one instance I will never forget. Between the two of us we found solutions for all of his fears. He moved himself forward when he felt comfortable and stopped being scared. He was most happy we had found a home for his rat too!

Like many people, I have a fear of failure. As I mentioned earlier, I felt like such a failure in university that when it came to writing this book I was very nervous and scared. I was fearful my colleagues would not like my book and would think I did not know what I was talking about. Before I even started the book I'd talked myself out of it! Finally, I just decided to bite the bullet and move forward with the book and I am so happy I was able to talk myself through my fear.

Negative Thoughts Can Create Self-Doubt

Self-doubt is another emotion that will creep in with negative thoughts. I personally have had a lot of self-doubt in the past. Of course a lot of this stems from low self-esteem and not feeling good about a lot of things in my life. I have sometimes felt I was not worthy of what I have.

This is false. I *am* worthy of where I am, what I do and what I have. You are also worthy of being where you are and what you do in your life. Keep reminding yourself of this and they are words you can live by. Keep up the positive self-talk. We all create our own realities in life and we deserve the good things that will come our way.

One of the areas I need to keep focused on is my weight. Time and time again, I have tried different ways to lose weight. Some I have self-sabotaged for one reason or another and others just didn't work. But, I believe that no matter what happens with my weight, it will not prevent me from moving forward in my life. I still continue with my workouts and joke around to everyone that I must be the fittest fat person you know. I may never get to my ultimate weight, but I am strong. And I do know exercise helps lower my stress level and makes me feel better, so I refuse to give that part of my life up. So the message is, don't worry about what people say or think and don't listen to your own negative self-talk; believe in what you are doing!

How to Prevent Negativity

So what do you do when negativity creeps into your life? You almost have to have a radio announcer saying things in your head to you and rewrite the script of your life. You want to stop yourself from focusing on the negative and self-doubt and start focusing on the *"You can"* attitude.

A great example of letting the negative and self-doubt creep in is when people follow a diet or exercise program and they cheat and eat sweets one day or miss a workout one day. It will not matter in the end. It does not mean you give up the whole program, it just means that tomorrow you try to do better. We will not always be perfect with these skills. We are rewriting the script. If you fall off the wagon seven times in a month, then try to make that mistake only five times next month.

The way to look at negativity in life is that you can change your ways one small step at a time. You are not going to be able to change every fear you have during every moment of your life. You need to take life one day at a time and one step at a time. Preparing yourself at the beginning of an activity or picturing yourself doing something you don't normally want to do and focusing on doing a small part with success is all you need to do at the beginning.

Right now think of a fear that is holding you back. Brainstorm ways around the fear and choose one of the strategies we've discussed above and see if you can move forward through this fear. Even one step is progress!

In some of Susan Jeffers' work she suggests that we need to use affirmations in our lives every day to help prevent the negativity from creeping in. She gives some suggested activities in her book, *Life is Huge*. It is amazing how you can push out the negative words and feelings by just restating your thinking. She states that the affirmations are strong positive messages that you need to help snap yourself out of the negative reverie you might find yourself in. She says, "... frequent repetition of ... simple positive statements has the power to relax our bodies, quiet our minds and allow us to see the brighter side of life. Amazing."[28]

Jeffers goes on to suggest different affirmations that will help us with our everyday lives. Some are simple and some are a little longer, but the underlying message is, change how we look at our lives and it is amazing how we can change how we feel about ourselves and our work.

"As you begin using your favorite affirmations, you will notice that little by little, the "habit" of thinking negatively will be replaced by the "habit" of thinking positively ... powerfully ... lovingly ... and peacefully."[29]

. . .

Points to Remember

▸ Fear and self-doubt
  - Everyone has fears; it is how we deal with them that counts

▸ Be careful not to preach to the client if you have been or are going through similar issues:
  - Remember feelings have no "time limit" and can surface when you least expect them to
  - One major moment in your life can change you— try to see the positives in these situations

▸ Fear can be a paralyzing emotion:
  - Don't let fear prevent you from realizing your dreams
  - You create your own reality in life
  - You deserve the good things that will come your way
  - Don't give any weight to the negative talk around you (or from within you!)

▸ Develop a *"You Can"* attitude

Chapter 7 Challenge & Activity

1. Positive Self-Talk

Think about the last time you had a day that everything went right for you and not one thing went wrong. If you can only think of a few or none at all, you are focusing on the negative side of your day and not the positive side. If you change how you look at the events of your day in a more positive light, then your outlook and demeanor tends to become more positive.

The challenge is to say five positive things to yourself every day for a week. Repeat these as many times as you feel necessary during the day to start believing they are true. After the week, review how your mood may have been different or the outlook of your day may have changed because you are starting off each day with positives then reminding yourself of the positives throughout the day.

A variation of the activity can be to reframe everything you do or say during the day to be more positive. The question lots of people ask is, "Is your glass half empty or half full?" If we can reframe how we view things into "learning experiences" or think good things can and will come out of even bad situations, then our whole demeanor changes. Some examples of reframing might be:

Negatives	Positives
You never do the dishes	Do you think it is possible to do the dishes today?
The client always complains about the same things everyday	Today I learned things my client was struggling with
The clerks never get anything right	Thank you for being honest about your mistake
We need to learn not to make so many mistakes on our reports	Why don't we get everyone to proofread reports for each other and check for errors before we hand them in?

2. Self-Visualization

Making time for self-visualization can help the body rejuvenate. In this activity you are going to practice how to use self-visualization. Using this technique can help you feel more focused and give you energy for times when you may need to move forward after mistakes. It is a great activity to do with clients who need to focus in their sessions or who cannot seem to relax when you are working with them.

Find yourself a quiet space where you can do some deep thinking without interruption. Do some deep breathing and slowly count to ten. Now visualize yourself as a child during a moment when you were happy. Remember those feelings. Now think about what you have always wanted to do or something you always dreamed of happening in your life. See yourself doing the activity or having that dream come true. After a few minutes of seeing this picture in your mind, write down or draw your vision. Ask yourself how you can attain this goal and what you need to do to get there. Now write down all the things you need to do to make your vision a reality, breaking them down into small steps. This may be more attainable than you first thought. If you focus energy into making good things happen to you it is amazing how your outlook may change in life.

You can also set goals using the self-visualization activity. The goal setting activity called "The Goal Setting Ladder," can be found in Chapter 10 and Appendix N.

8

Laughter Is the Best Medicine

In the helping profession, you really need to learn how to laugh. I don't mean telling jokes in the way of laughing at others. I interpret humour as being able to find the light side of yourself and the situations you find yourself in. If you cannot laugh at yourself then you are not enjoying life in general. You don't have to be a funny person; you just don't have to take yourself too seriously. There is humour surrounding us everywhere, if we look for it.

Humour can be used to make us feel better, help relieve stress, lighten the mood in a room and can help us stay positive in our lives. But there are caveats.

Don't Take a Prank Too Far

There aren't many black and white answers when it comes to working with other people. You do the best you can do with the tools you are given. When I think back to my first years teaching, I had a lot of fun because I surrounded myself with people who could enjoy themselves too. I specifically remember one time on April Fools' Day a group of us came in early and decided to play a trick on my neighbouring colleague who was a very popular English teacher. He had a great bond with the students and the staff. We came in that morning and had rearranged his classroom so that it was reversed! When he came in he had a good laugh.

The second thing that happened that day was a similar prank on another colleague who taught across the hall from me. He was a great mentor teacher and was always willing to help me when I was trying to get lessons organized. Some students had come in the night before and rearranged many things in his classroom. If there was one thing he liked the most, it was that he knew where everything was in his room exactly where he had left it the previous day. He was not as amused as our first colleague was.

The first prank, which I was responsible for, got blamed on the grade 12 students. The second teacher however, thought I had done his room up for him and he continually let me know he was going to get me back. He would tell everyone I had wrecked things in his room. When students were getting in trouble for being in the hall during class time, he would tell them to say they were from my class so the administration would blame me for having so many students in the hall. Well this was getting ridiculous, so in all good fun, I let a student out in the hall when they were not supposed to during tutorial to get a book. I told him to say he was from the Italian teacher's room if he got caught. Well the principal came into the room with the student five minutes later and asked, "Did you tell this student that he could go to his locker to get a text book and if he got caught to say he was from Mr.—'s classroom?"

Being my second year of teaching, you could imagine what thoughts were running through my head. What am I going to say? How am I going to get out of this? The pranking had gone too far. In the end, my best play at that point was honesty, so I replied, "Yes."

For a moment my principal looked at me with a serious look and I thought I was in for it. Worse yet, it was right in front of my students and I was trying desperately to have them respect me even though I was so young. Finally, after what seemed to be an eternity, he cracked a smile and started to laugh. He told me I should be a little more careful next time. Whew—saved by a funny bone!

At that point I decided the pranks were over and it was time to come clean. Both men were in good spirits about this—especially since I brought everyone treats.

However, one thing to take from this is we have to be careful our pranks or attempts at humour do not go too far. In the moment, my pranks did not seem like they were hurting anyone—but often we can't foresee where a prank can lead or what buttons they may push emotionally in others. Thus, I am not telling everyone to go out and start pranking people, what I am saying is to enjoy yourself at work and look for light-hearted moments.

Be prepared to laugh at yourself. You are most likely a funny individual and you don't even know it. It is better to not take the chance of hurting other people's feelings so if you are able to poke fun of yourself, then you are most likely not going to offend others. The trick is to keep it in good spirits, with good intentions. You will also get some good laughs out of it too.

Humour Pitfalls

Some people find humour in teasing. This is not the best way to maintain relationships, especially in the workplace, because people can definitely lose sight of the humour or may take offense to comments made. If you are going to use teasing as a type of humour, be cautious. Never tease about a trait or gender bias; we are all sensitive to this type of teasing and it can easily be taken the wrong way.

As Polly Shulman wrote in her article "Crack Me Up: Breaking the Humor Code," there is a line that can be crossed quite easily because "... humor is very much in the eye of the beholder, and what's intended as a witty remark may fall miserably flat or even seem cruel in the context of a difficult or imbalanced relationship."[30] Thus when we find humour in situations that others don't find funny, we have to be careful we are not offending people. As well, people can often repeat jokes they think are funny but other people might not. When you are just trying to be social, you could end up alienating yourself—which would definitely defeat the intended purpose of having a good sense of humour!

Another good point regarding humour brought up in Shulman's article was that, "Almost every sweet, supportive way of using it has an evil twin; an aggressive, selfish or manipulative version."[31] Thus even well-intentioned humour can backfire on us. We have to be careful to not fall into this trap. When used correctly the effects can be positive and enjoyable, but when used negatively humour can have the opposite effect. When used correctly, humour puts your life in perspective and you are able to have a more positive outlook.

Humour Heals

Find someone who will make you laugh or try to find humour in the most stressful situations. Laughing almost always makes you feel better. More and more, even the medical profession embraces the power of positivity and laughter in helping people to heal. When I was in the hospital waiting room to take some tests, I overheard a conversation between a patient and her mother. They were laughing and carrying on about the funny things that can happen in a hospital. Later on, I found out that the younger person had a severe illness and she was not given a very good prognosis. Her mother stated to me before I left, "Find humour in your situation because you will go to sleep at night with a lighter heart!"

This person did feel better and although she eventually lost her battle to her disease, she lived a year longer than expected. Her family really believes it was the positive attitude she had and the humour she found in her everyday life that made the difference. Also when they remember her, what they remember the most is the smile that she always had and the laughter they shared.

Humour Is All Around Us—We Just Need to Look

Some hospitals are not set up well at all. A friend and I went to see a sick person in the hospital and it took us at least twenty minutes to find the room. There was construction going on and they were doing repairs from a flood. By the time we got to see our friend, we had little time left to visit. Then when we went to leave the building we thought we would be smart and follow the map. So off we went following the appropriate lines on the floor and the map. We ended up in the psych ward where they lock all the doors so no one can pass through. As we were back tracking on the map I started giggling and said, "I am a pretty educated person with a degree and I cannot find my way out of the hospital. What does this say about me?"

My friend replied, "I have two degrees and a masters and I can't find my way out either. What does this say about me?"

I responded with, "That makes you worse!"

We laughed for a good five minutes. I still tell this story at times and laugh about our situation. We could have gotten angry or been upset that we were going around in circles, but instead we found humour in the situation and made fun of ourselves. Life can get very stressful and if you don't find humour in awkward or difficult situations then you will spend a whole lot of time being angry or upset. That is not a good use of your time.

Being able to find humour in awful situations takes some work because life can throw some pretty bad curve balls your way. One time I was dealing with some very horrific abuse that had happened to a student at the hands of an adult in the community. I was interviewed by the authorities and at the conclusion of the interview we had a candid conversation about our jobs. I cannot disclose his specific job due to confidentiality, but suffice it to say not many people could deal with the amount of information this person had to process daily. I told him that I admire him for the job he does because I could never do his job. He turned to me with a smile and said he could never be a teacher of teenagers and he admired me for doing my job, which I found surprising. The second thing he stated was that he loves to watch comedy shows and laugh every day after work because he said laughter helped him deal with the stress and made his mood better at home with his family.

Finding Others Who Are Funny

A few years ago my mother took me to see a panel of women at The Power of Women conference.[32] There were many great speakers but a few really stood out for me. The first was Jessica Holmes, a comedian, author and motivational speaker from Ottawa, Ontario. (As we share the same last name I thought that she had to be great before we even saw her!) She was the Master of Ceremonies and she warmed up and entertained the crowd between each speaker. She was absolutely hilarious and I laughed so hard my stomach hurt. A quote from her website says it best, "As a Motivational Speaker and Comedian, my passion is to help you reignite your spark, achieve your goals and dreams, and laugh all the way to the bank/ trailer park/ dolphin training facility, or wherever else you spend your time. The point is: life is awesome! Let's enjoy it!"[33]

Another great speaker that day was Marlee Matlin, an academy award winning actress who lost her hearing at a young age. She spoke about how many people don't understand how to talk to deaf people. She poked fun of herself and others for trying to talk to her even though they knew she was deaf. I really admire her for her tenacity to continue to move forward and not let her hearing impairment stop her from obtaining all of her dreams, and she spoke about it in the most humourous way. We can learn a lot from anyone who finds humour in a difficult situation!

Finally my favourite two speakers that day were Loretta LaRoche and the main speaker—Ellen DeGeneres. Ellen stated that she loves what she does because it is important, when things are not going well, to laugh. This was her gift to people; to help them deal with the growing issues they were facing everyday by having some time away from their problems and laughing. It was her dream to take away the stress and strain of their lives and hopefully make them laugh their troubles away for short periods of time.

Loretta LaRoche, an acclaimed speaker, author, and international stress manager and humour consultant,[34] spoke about how we need to poke fun of our daily lives to deal with stress. She suggested we picture ourselves in our own comedy series and imagine we are the main star. Well, I can tell you, many days I don't feel like my life is a comedy series, but I can find humourous things that do happen. Some days when I am working, weird things can happen which are stressful but I can find some nugget of humour from them.

Many people would not find this funny, but there was a year that I had three floods in my office. The first one destroyed most of the stuff in the office and the other two, although not as big, did do some damage. I came in one day and said that I am going to get hip-waders to wear to work so I can work through the next flood. This was not the best situation, but lightening the moment helped.

Laughter = Stress Relief

Laughter can reduce stress in so many different ways; I constantly need to remind myself that it is important to laugh every day. Sometimes we need to be the catalyst to make other people laugh or to lighten up the mood in the room a bit. At work, we decided to focus in on one thing each staff member did well in the year and make a poster honouring them for it. We had one staff member who was going through some health issues and seemed a little down. On a Friday when she was away we made a poster calling her employee of the month, complete with her photo on it. Well it did the trick! When she came back the following Monday, and saw the poster, she had a huge smile on her face. Plus everyone congratulated her all day which made her smile and laugh. It let her focus on something else for a short period of time to relieve the stress that had built up in her life.

Another colleague stated that we needed to post the emergency number by the phone. We pointed out to him that it was already posted by the main classroom phone. When he turned to the sign—which was neon orange and not tiny—he asked how long that had been there because he did not remember seeing it. I told him for the past two years. He finally said he did not have one in his office and he wanted one. Well he was away one day, so we posted 17 bright yellow signs all over his bulletin board so we made sure he knew how to call 9-1-1. I don't know who had the best laugh over this situation, us or him.

Many people would not understand my sense of humour if they did not know the intricacies of my job. There was one time I was in a curling tournament and we were in a final game. None of us were doing well, and someone on my team asked me to tell her a joke to lighten up the mood and make her focus on something else. I said what I would find funny I don't think you would find funny! That did make her laugh. I did state that we are out here in the finals, losing badly, curling badly and everyone else is having a serious game. I found that funny. We were in a lousy situation and not playing well, so we all needed a good laugh. This proves the point that you can help yourself out of stressful situations using laughter. We did start curling a bit better when we loosened up and relaxed. We didn't win, but our overall performance in the entire tournament was pretty good and we had fun.

Laughter Can Help Ease the Pain

So how do you do this when you are having a crazy hectic day? I truly believe there is always a brighter side to crazy and hectic. I worked with a great team of people and I remember one day I found out some terrible news about a child who was diagnosed with terminal cancer at age two. I was very sad and felt helpless because I could not help the parents deal with their situation. I could not help them with the pain and suffering they were going to endure. We had a pretty good work day with the students and afterwards we were having our staff meeting. I remember there was a substitute in that day and she was asking us questions about our students. What helped me was that we started telling stories of different things that had happened throughout the program and how crazy some of our days could get. We laughed so hard at the different situations and as we told more stories they seemed to get funnier by the minute.

It was the best therapy I could have ordered that day. I laughed so hard that my stomach hurt and I was crying. I really needed to laugh hard that day because I was so sad. I was sad for my friends and how they were going through such a horrible period in their lives. As Ellen DeGeneres said, sometimes people need to lose their problems for an hour a day. We, as Helpers, sometimes need to do the same.

If you think back throughout the past month or two, I am sure you can find a few examples where things might have been so crazy in your day that they were funny. I suggest writing them down because you never know when you will need that pick-me-up. As we were telling stories of times that were the most bizarre and hilarious of our careers, I was reminding myself that we need to write this material down so that when I am angry or frustrated, I can remind myself of that good laugh and brighten my mood up. As well, don't forget a little distraction of laughter may not solve any problems, but it can brighten up those tough times to help you deal with life in general.

. . .

Points to Remember

- Humour is everywhere—remember to look for it!

- Be careful of humour pitfalls
  - There can be a negative side to humour if not used in an appropriate manner
  - Teasing is one type of humour you have to be careful of—remember to:
    - Choose your subject carefully
    - Don't use gender teases

- Don't take pranks too far or at the expense of others

- Humour can heal and help relieve stress
  - Remember to laugh every day
    - Makes you feel happier
    - Lightens your mood

For some resources on Humour, please see Appendix M.

Chapter 8 Challenge & Activity

1. Develop a Laughter Journal

At the end of your day, think about something funny that happened to you. See how this can change a negative feeling into a more positive one by focusing on the funny things that happened. Keep a laughter journal of events to refer back to on those long days. It is amazing how situations can remain funny over time. Share your stories with colleagues and friends. It can be very entertaining for everyone involved.

2. You're a Star!

Using self-visualization, imagine yourself on stage telling jokes to colleagues where you are the star lighting up the entire room. It is a great feeling to have a good laugh and turn the negative into a positive. You don't have to share with other people in person, but imagine they all feel you are knocking their socks off. The beauty of self-visualization is that it doesn't matter if other people may not think of it as being funny, only you need to find it funny. Laughing as much as possible will help to keep you feeling good at the end of a long day.

9

Knowing Yourself

Now we'll look at the personal side of what makes a person stand out or makes them unique in their line of work, and how we can use this unique quality to make our lives better and to help the people around us to see the best of themselves.

As Helpers, we are individuals who have chosen a profession that can be emotionally challenging. Topics that will be explored in this chapter include limits, treating all situations as learning experiences and remembering to share the lessons you learn. You will become a more effective Helper and you will also benefit from listening to that inner voice when it tells you you've had enough.

You need to understand what success means to you and celebrate that. This will help with all aspects of life, if you can define and understand where you want to go and start working on how to get there. Only you can set and manage this goal for yourself.

Reaching Our Limits

We need to understand when we have reached our limits. I remember when I was working in a bylaw department for one of our local municipalities. Now if you want to learn a lot of patience, work in the bylaw department of any city. Everyone has an opinion of you and anyone who gets a ticket likes to come and complain or blame you for all the bad stuff in their life. It can be entertaining at times, especially if you are a people watcher like me, but other times you can focus on or start adopting the negativity for yourself.

I will never forget this one phone call I received. The person at the other end of the phone was very angry with a citation he had received and he asked me what my name was, which I told him. I was only a temporary clerk and new in this role, so I was trying to do the best job I could to impress my boss. As the conversation continued he threatened me, and threatened to have me fired. He was starting to get under my skin. I took the verbal abuse for at least five minutes until I finally passed along the phone call to my manager.

This phone call upset me on multiple levels. First of all, I should have transferred the phone call to my manager well before I did. I was trying so hard to be perfect that while my inner voice was telling me it was time to let the person go, I continued to let him go on and berate me instead of asking for help. Secondly, I let him get under my skin and started to let what he was saying to me sink in. He was bullying me verbally because he thought I had the power to get him out of the citation. When my manager talked to me about it I was so close to tears that he told me to take a walk and come back.

I learned several lessons that day. It does not make you weak to ask for help from people. That is why we have managers or principals. I should have asserted my personal boundaries and asked the caller to phone back when he calmed down because no one should have to be harassed and no one deserves to be yelled at for anything let alone a ticket I did not issue. Finally, if I had just walked away and taken a break I would not have lost it at work. These were all good lessons. As a Helper, you need to know when it is time for you to take a break and/or take yourself out of a stressful situation.

All Situations Are Learning Experiences

It is good to look at situations as learning experiences. Some jobs you have may not be your preference, but every experience you have will help you move forward into the next part of your life. The job in the by-law department helped prepare me for the stressful meetings I have in my current career and for the stress of deadlines as well.

You have to know when to walk away and calm yourself down. It is important that you, as a Helper, take the time to collect your thoughts if you need to, and that you make this clear to the people you work with. An example of this was when I was supervising a school-wide English exam. At that time in my career, I was working as a learning support teacher where we would help out students who had difficulties in class or who had a learning disability and qualified for adaptations for exams or assignments. One of our students purposely skipped school and chose not to write the exam so, as per procedure, we contacted the parents to let them know. I called and left a message. About an hour and a half later, the student's mother showed up while we had thirty or so students writing this exam in my classroom. She was angry and kept yelling at me and blaming me for ruining her day because I could not keep her son in class.

I must say I was absolutely stunned. I called out of courtesy and the protocols of our department. This parent was so upset about the situation that she had taken it upon herself to come in while the other students were still writing their exams!

The previous training I had was a blessing because I was able to react in the opposite way than this parent wanted me to. She was saying some pretty hurtful things and luckily, other staff heard her and escorted her down to the office to talk to the administration for me so I could continue with the test. Unfortunately, the students were upset about what happened and needed help to calm down to finish the exam.

What I did not like about the situation was the timing of the debrief. The administration was so concerned about how I was going to handle the situation they wanted to discuss it right then and there. That was their agenda. I just wanted to continue to help my students finish writing their exams so I could move on with my day. Processing situations right away are good for most but not for me. I like to think about what I am going to say to someone. If I start talking about a situation when I am angry, the anger will get worse. If I have learned anything in my life, it is that I need processing and calming time. But they did not take into consideration how I felt about it and did not pay attention to what I needed in that moment.

As you can see, all situations are learning experiences. If you can set boundaries with your colleagues and ask them to respect the fact that you need some time to deal with a situation personally, then you are making room for your needs. Being assertive is the key. Looking back, I wish I had handled it by saying, "I appreciate the fact that you are concerned, however, I would like a little bit of time to get everything settled down in my classroom. Then I would like to take a five minute break to gather myself. Thanks." This way I would have been clear about what I needed without disregarding the fact that they wanted to talk. Working on a script after the fact will prepare you for the next time something similar could happen to you.

Learning how to deal with people who are angry is a skill every Helper can use, and should be added to your repertoire. A goal that would have been good for the department to establish after this situation was to contact parents at the end of the day so they would not have the opportunity to come in during an exam again. One of the changes we did make was to ensure we locked our door during exams so no uninvited guests would be able to access the room. There are always opportunities to turn negative experiences into learning experiences.

I needed to embrace the fact that my students respected and cared for me and they did not want someone coming into my room and harming me even if it was only verbally. As well, being able to see this situation from this parent's point of view was sad because she was having a difficult time with her child. How horrible that must have been for her.

As my sister always says, mistakes are just lessons we need to learn at that moment of time. This is a good way to look at life. You need to learn from and share the lessons with others if and when they may be willing to listen to them, just as I am sharing the lessons I have learned with you.

Setting Goals

I am constantly asking students to set short- and long-term goals for themselves. One day I thought maybe it was time I set some goals too. So I started setting goals and then envisioning what my life would be like if I obtained these dreams. I revisit this exercise often; it helps me focus on and prepare for what I want to accomplish personally and professionally.

Setting goals will help you to move forward with your life. Plus if your goals are written down and given a timeline, then you are more apt to accomplish them and to hold yourself accountable when you aren't. Another way to help yourself accomplish your goals is to reward yourself with something once the goal is accomplished. Rewards help to keep you on track. (See goal setting activity at the end of the chapter.)

Another thing goal setting does is help define priorities. Cheryl Richardson discusses this topic. Her main premise in the book, *Take Time for Your Life*, is fully visible in her title. Analyze how you spend your time, define what your priorities are, and if necessary, adjust your focus. We all have busy lives and it can be difficult to fit everything in. Thus we need to consider wisely how we will spend our time. It is easy to spend time working outside of work. All the new technology out there—cell phones, email, laptops—make work available to us at all hours of the day, wherever we may be. So what is a priority for you? Richardson states there are three things you need to keep your priorities straight: looking realistically at how you spend your time, asking yourself if these priorities make sense (and possibly changing them) and honouring your priorities once they are set. In her words, "By following your inner wisdom, you'll intentionally reorder your priorities or set new ones so that you can shift your focus and attention to what's important."[35]

The next time someone does something or schedules something for you that does not fit with your priorities, be assertive and take back your life. You will not regret the decision.

Acknowledge Yourself

It is important to understand the areas we may find difficult in our work. We all have them. Thinking we know everything is both unrealistic and even arrogant. We may know more now than we did before, but we still do not have all the answers for every situation.

A strategy that may be helpful is to take situations that may be challenging for you and make them into goals you want to accomplish. This is taking some negative things in your life and changing them into positives or learning situations. Let's face it, there are areas everyone needs to work on in their lives so instead of always doing the same thing, focus on change and embrace the positive feelings that come from changing yourself for the better. Then spend some time celebrating the small triumphs.

I find it ironic that I spend a lot of time trying to boost the self-esteem of clients and celebrating their victories and triumphs but I can still sometimes forget to do this for myself. As a Helper, there is nothing more satisfying than helping clients and observing a break through or an "a-ha" moment where they begin to change their lives. This is a natural high in life and these are the greatest highs I have ever experienced. And if these positive experiences or movements forward are what you ask your clients to hang onto, then why don't you hang on to them as a Helper? If you can take the time to acknowledge your good work, then it changes your outlook on the work you do.

After having many rewarding years in the teaching profession, I know I need to continue to keep listening to myself. When I am too tired to work out or my body is complaining it needs a break, I am much better about listening to it. It is a shame if we spend so much time working to help other people but we spend little time working to help ourselves. I know there are times in life when I need quiet time. Having a healthier me is important because when my clients need to have all of my attention to get them through a crisis, I will be there for them.

Listening to Your Inner Voice

Remembering to take a step back and assess situations can help save us from misery later on. When helping people, we need to read the signs our body, mind or life is throwing at us.

One time I did not slow down and listen to my inner voice, and I became a hazard to my own health. I slipped while doing a practice slide in curling and broke my shoulder. It was the most painful injury I had ever experienced. I did not slow down and did not take any time off at first because I felt it would not be fair to my new teaching partner who had just started that year. About one month into the injury, my shoulder socket was continuing to make ominous cracking noises when I would move it too much.

I had a hairline fracture which meant that as long as I slowed down and rested, the socket would heal itself, and I could avoid surgery. Stupid me, I kept going; I continued to do what I did before the injury, including going to the gym and maintaining my workload. I had a follow-up doctor's appointment and he must have suspected I was not getting the proper rest. He finally asked me how I got there. When I replied that I'd driven he chastised me gently about not giving myself time to heal.

You know yourself and your body. Your muscles ache when you over-do things. If they ache longer than a few days after going to the gym or doing a physical activity, then damage may have been done and they need a period of healing before continuing to do more exercise. There were times when I would push myself and get injured and set myself back in my training for months. It has been a hard lesson for me, because working out is a way I relieve stress. To take things easy is difficult, but I've had to learn to ease up when necessary.

Another big lesson I learned is that I only had to ask my work partner to help me more. It was that easy. When looking at the work load, we both need to split the burden, and we both need to do our fair share. But there are times when one or the other of us will be working a little harder or do more to cover if one of us is not feeling well. When I finally asked for help easing my workload temporarily, he did just fine learning the ropes of the program and class quickly and competently. I am not irreplaceable and sometimes others can bring more life to a program or work with kids on new skills or ideas that I have not thought of. We are all unique in our own way and it is presumptive of us to think we are the only ones who can do our jobs.

Knowing What Success Means to You

We are better people when we have confidence in what we are doing at work. When we feel confident, this is a feeling we should focus on.

Be sure to take the time to reflect on what you want and what you may need. This focus can help you attain your dreams and move forward to a life you want to lead. As well, knowing when to slow down or what you need to make sure your life is complete is an important aspect of life. This is not just for people who are in the helping profession. Only you are in control of yourself and thus you are the expert on you. Working to achieve what you need and being sure to listen to those needs will help make you a well-rounded Helper.

. . .

Points to Remember

- Know your limitations
    - Know when to assert them
    - Acknowledging limitations does not make you weak, it makes you smart

- We can learn from all situations and experiences
    - Look back and analyze how you could better prepare for next time
    - Remember to be assertive and set boundaries

- Set short- and long-term goals
    - Set timelines and review them
    - Be flexible enough to adjust timelines along the way
    - Understand what your priorities are

- Listen to your inner voice
    - Especially if it is telling you to:
        - Start making some changes
        - Take better care of yourself

- Understand what success means to you and reach for it

Chapter 9 Challenge & Activity

1. What you Want and What You Need

Take a step back and look at all the things you are doing. Do you feel everything is attainable? Try doing a few less activities this week and look at how you are feeling. Was it better when you were doing less? Is there anything you have wanted to do and are not getting done? Look at what other activities you might drop to make sure you are accomplishing everything you would like to accomplish in your day. You may be able to find extra time to do something you have always wanted to do. What is important to you?[36]

2. Developing and Achieving Your Goals

A good way to achieve your goals is to think of them backwards. For example, think about what you want to achieve as the end goal or the top rung of a ladder. Now think of all the smaller steps you can break your goal down into. These are the other steps of the Goal Setting Ladder. Some people use pyramids, others just a table but I always like to have a visual of what I am working towards. Whichever method you choose, when you make yourself accountable and develop appropriate timelines, you will be well on your way to achieving your goals. (See Appendix N for a template.)

"Visit" or look at where you are on the ladder; when reviewing a goal it is important to hold yourself accountable for your actions. If you are well on your way to obtaining what you want in life, great, keep up the good work! If you are struggling to achieve your goals then maybe the goals were too difficult or unachievable. You need to have realistic expectations when working in your profession and if you don't make sure you are being realistic then you will stretch yourself too thin. Sometimes you may need to revise your goals or rework them so they are more attainable. This is why it is important to review your goals regularly, because there may be patterns you can find as to why you are not achieving them. This information is invaluable when trying to figure out why a particular goal may not be working or be attainable right away.

Finally when you do achieve one of your goals, celebrate! Treat yourself to a night out with friends or an extra date night with your significant other or a day at the spa; whatever "celebrating" means to you. But you're not done yet—after achieving a goal, revisit your goal list and tackle the next one. Or set new goals. Not only is it healthy for you to continue to move ahead on your own journey in life, you will also be able to teach your clients similar methods to keep moving forward in their lives.

10

The Gifts

Throughout my career, I have had some touching moments. These are moments that I refer to as "gifts" I've received, because they've truly touched my heart and made a positive impact on me emotionally. These moments create positive energy within us so we can push on and fight for those that need fighting for. Instead of remembering the people who get under our skin, what can get us through the bleakest days are those who touch our hearts and change our lives.

While looking at the gifts you've received remember that these positive gains will help keep you going when things in your life may not be so positive. Embrace clients or students who are different and see how they can bring life to a group or classroom. Recognize that challenges can be gifts and opportunities can present themselves through adversity. Here are a few "gifts" I would like to share with you, from people who have taught me more than I ever taught them.

Terminal Illness

Michael J. Fox, an actor and author originally from Burnaby, British Columbia, who now resides in New York, describes his life as a gift. Fox suffers from Parkinson's disease.[37] He has written two autobiographies and is very candid about his life and how he has to live with this disease. He describes himself as an incurable optimist. It is his positive attitude and making sure that he enjoys every moment of his life that has helped him get through the tougher challenges:

> For everything this disease has taken, something with greater value has been given—sometimes just a marker that points me in a new direction that I might not otherwise have traveled. So, sure, it may be one step forward and two steps back, but after a time with Parkinson's, I've learned that what is important is making that one step count; always looking up.[38]

I had a student in a similar situation. He has taught me many lessons. This student had Duchene muscular dystrophy. This terminal disease first attacks the muscles, then progresses to cause skeletal deformations of the body. Basically, the mind is fine but the body stops working.[39] He struggled with day to day activities and routines we often take for granted, for example getting dressed in the morning. However, he did not complain about the hand he had been dealt in life. He continued to wake up on the bright side every morning and discussed his life with a positive attitude.

I will never forget having a bad day, trying to convince one student to finish his assignment and having another teacher not understand why it took wheelchair students forty-five minutes to go to the bathroom. I was mad and upset when talking about this with my student Rob (this is not his real name). He told me I should not worry about it so much. He said he has to deal with people not understanding his life all the time and he and his dad have had a lot of fun over the years teasing these people. He asked me not to worry about him so much and he knows if anything bad went on in the school, I would always be there for him. That just touched my heart.

I will never forget the day I had to tell him I was leaving the school to take on a different job. He was then in Grade 11. I had worked with him for four years. We had a final meeting and tears started welling up in both our eyes. I told him he was ready for me to go and he would be fine. He said, I know, because you have taken care of me so well. Then he gave me one of the best gifts a teacher could get, a little angel that had the words "thank you" stitched on it. He told me I had been his angel and had prepared him for life beyond high school. Teachers' pride in our jobs is dependent on how well the students do. This student gave me the opportunity to leave and feel good about it; he told me I had done my job well.

Unfortunately just after Rob's 19th Birthday he lost his battle with Duchene muscular dystrophy. He was so special because he was able to pack more into his short life than many people do in a lifetime. He lived every day like it was his last and he was able to touch other people's hearts too. Many people could learn from him; I know I did. He has always reminded me to live life to the fullest no matter how crazy it gets.

Happy Wall of Memories

Another great thing you can do is create a "happy wall" or "memory wall". Surround yourself with positive things reminding you of good times during your career. The notes that students, clients, colleagues, supervisors, friends etc., give you to remind you of when things would go right or the notes of encouragement you've received over time. It is amazing how much better you will feel looking at these pictures and notes on the wall. When you are having those days where nothing seems right and clients are struggling, a happy wall can be a much-needed boost. (Refer to the activity at the end of this chapter for further details and to create your own wall of memories)

My daughter had a great Kindergarten teacher who came up with an idea for parents who had a difficult time leaving their children in class. She had the students trace their hands and then they cut them out to give to their parents. They also kissed the hand several times so that when the parents got lonely and missed them, they could put the cut-out hand to their faces and receive a kiss. What a brilliant idea! My daughter's hand had a place on my wall for years. And, I would tell my high school students what it was so they would know I was also a mother who had feelings. I don't know how many times I would pull that off the wall and up to my face or I would just look at it and remind myself of the important things in life. Many times the smile I was having a hard time finding would return. It truly helped me forward so I could look for solutions instead of focusing on problems.

When Youth Act like Adults

It is a great feeling when youth show empathy. One time my students and I were out in the community at a new trampoline park. This was an awesome adventure for our young adults and they were able to play basketball, jump against the walls, play dodge ball and jump into a foam pit.

They dared me to jump into the foam pit and of course, I decided I was up for the challenge. Well, jumping in was no problem but getting out was another story. I ended up getting stuck inside because I kept losing a sock and I would move the foam around so that I was sinking to the bottom. Two of the young adults came over and tried to help me out of the pit. They got pulled back in trying to help me. I did not know whether to laugh or cry. They were trying to help me out of a pretty embarrassing moment. Here were these young adults who struggled with making positive choices in their lives, trying to help me out of a sticky situation. I was so proud of them!

When changes are recognizable in young people, we have to cherish and celebrate their accomplishment. Over the years, I have seen many of my students become young adults. They have shared many gifts with our staff. When they have made positive choices in their lives, we feel pride for being able to be a small factor in helping facilitate this change.

Thanks can come in many forms and one is finding out that a client you helped comes out of terrible situation to function in society.

Extra Energy Needs Nurturing Not Discipline

I had one student in particular that would brighten up my day every day he attended school. On the one hand, he had so much energy that

I felt tired every time he would speak—some days he was a significant challenge to work with, but on the other hand, he breathed life into our program. I will never forget the times we had with him when we were out in the community. He had never previously had many opportunities to do simple activities such as golfing, playing pool or experiencing museums. We were able to open up new doors for him and in turn, he gave his gift of life and energy back to us tenfold.

Two different events come to mind and make me smile when I think of this student. One time we were at the flight museum and of course, he was so full of energy. We were walking around on our tour when he came up to me and said, "Debbie! I bet you can't do this!" He then proceeded to run ahead and jump to click his heels together. Unfortunately he did not jump high enough and he tripped, did a somersault and jumped back up all in the span of 10 seconds. He came running back to me and I said, smiling, "You're right. I don't think I could ever do that."

The second event happened when we were at the driving range and the students were learning to hit their way through a bucket of balls. This same student would always try to have competitions with me, and not being the best athlete, I did not really have a good track record of winning very many of these challenges. Anyway, he asked whether, if he could get the ball to hit the trampoline that was 125 yards away, I would take them for coffee.

So the competition began. After watching him for a few minutes I told him I thought my money was quite safe. He finished his bucket without hitting the trampoline but then to his delight, I gave him a few extra balls. He continued to miss. Finally I gave him my last three balls. On the final ball, he ended up hitting the trampoline.

I have never seen someone so excited! He was jumping up and down as if he won the lottery. At this particular driving range—like many others—you are supposed to be quiet to respect all of the other golfers. We were definitely not quiet that day. He gave everyone a high five and told them I had to take them all for coffee. The way he made me laugh and the excitement he brought to everyone that day was worth however much the coffee cost. This was a huge gift.

Taking the time to do activities with clients can be fun and rewarding. This may not work with all clients, but having the ability to change environments may produce positive results. In this case this student's enthusiasm to embrace a new activity, work at it, not give up and, ultimately, find success was what helped him to move forward—and all for the price of a cup of coffee. Look for ways to nurture the positives of the people you work with and it may rub off on you and make your days full of more enjoyment.

Gifts Can Come Later

I believe in my heart that the biggest impact we make as professionals is not always recognized right away. I have moved around a lot in my career and sometimes people take you for granted so it is not until you leave a position that they recognize the gifts you gave them. It is amazing how this happens. This is a great feeling when people miss you because once again this tells you, you have done a good job.

It is not just with colleagues. Clients can do this too. Success will sometimes happen later when a client realizes the changes you helped them to make. You don't really know when you have touched someone, but years later they may come back or they start working in the same profession and you see them again and you find out the impact you made on their lives. I have had a couple of students come back and tell me much later—ten years in one case—how much I had influenced them and how they are aspiring to emulate my style of teaching. Sometimes, as Helpers, we unknowingly plant seeds for which it is not until much later that we see our results in full bloom.

People often forget to tell others how they feel until it is too late. One way to find out how you are doing is to ask. One simple question can help you determine if you are on the right path as a Helper.

Compliments are infectious. When you give a person a compliment, it is amazing how people will start to reciprocate quickly. Don't wait until you leave a job to find out how you are doing or to compliment one of your colleagues, because they may be feeling the same way you are.

The Power of a Hug

We are taught not to touch students and rightly so, but sometimes there is so much anger or hurt in a teenager when they are talking to you or giving into emotions and crying, all you want to do is give them a hug. Many of the students I have worked with over the years have given into this urge and I have accepted, albeit cautiously at times. There are times that there is so much communicated in that hug that no words have to be spoken. These are the truly cherished moments in a career.

One particular time, a student had been working with me for four years. He was one of the angriest people I had ever encountered. There were times when I did not know what to say to him as he would come into my office and vent about what had happened and it was truly horrible stuff that would keep me awake at night worrying about him. This young man really did have every justification for being angry. When working with anger I know that what underlies this behaviour is pain. The pain this young man was in was heartbreaking.

We had many discussions punctuated by much swearing on his part—I didn't think I could learn any more choice words for my vocabulary but apparently I still had much to learn—and if I made a mistake in my sessions with him, boy would I find out about it. Through all of this time and the stress of the long discussions there were a lot of tears. His journey over the years at school was a long, difficult one.

When it was time for him to graduate I was so proud of all the changes he had made in his life. He'd worked on his disposition and anger issues and got himself off hard drugs. These were huge accomplishments, and along the way, he'd grown up too. At graduation, I told him he had taught me more than I had taught him and that just like the Bruno Mars song states, "You are amazing, just the way you are." I really truly believe that to this day.

After the ceremony, he had to wait a long time to talk to me. He patiently waited 40 minutes until I was alone and we had a quiet moment to say goodbye. He walked up to me with tears in his eyes and gave me the longest hug. He was shaking. I remember feeling all the thanks he was giving me in that moment and I knew he understood everything we had worked on together as a teacher and a student. I whispered in his ear that everything I had said was true, that he taught me more than I had taught him. During this hug I realized he might not have the words to express himself to me, but this was his poignant way of thanking me for everything I had done.

Using Observation Skills, You Can See Thankfulness

We don't always need verbal language to express emotion or gratitude. With good observation skills and an astute sense of what is going on around you, you can understand what your clients are telling you. We each in our own ways are trying to survive this work world. Yes, your choices have been maybe a little more positive, but that is what keeps us employed, not judging clients or students. We are employed to teach and guide them.

It is important not to be too arrogant about this. We need to be humble. I truly believe I was meant to help guide students and (now) adults to change, and I also believe that through hard work and dedication these people will blossom and shine. But I also realize I am only one Helper and I am replaceable by another who has similar motivations and skills. The way one person does something is not always the way I would do it but it does not mean it is wrong or bad. There have been times when I was away or one of my colleagues was away and we have had substitute teachers. We were able to learn many new tricks of the trade or they would think of some strategies we had not thought of. This was another gift.

Look around and find the gifts that already exist. There might be more in store for you than you thought.

Challenges = Gifts

Another way to look at things that happen in life is that each challenge is a gift. A great example of this was when I lost a job I never ever thought I would lose. I was doing a job where I was developing programs and tracking learning disabled students through trades programs. Teachers are part of a union and there are rules that need to be followed, so if more than one person is qualified for a position, it would then go by seniority. I actually thought mine was pretty good and I did a good job so I never ever thought I would not get this job back the following year. I poured my heart and soul into this position. But instead, another person with more seniority got the job for the next school year instead of me.

At first, it was impossible for me to view this event as a gift. It sure didn't feel like one! But it was. The gift I received in the end was another position, one where I was even happier. While it is a powerful gift to see a student who has rough beginnings succeed, I also believe gifts come to us in other, unexpected ways. My career has changed and progressed over the years and writing this book would have never come about had I not lost that job.

A second gift that going to a new program gave me was being able to be part of the community through different projects. These were opportunities I would not have had if I would have stayed at the first job. We have to learn that opportunities present themselves out of adversity and we need to make sure we focus on those. I needed to be open to trying something new because of my circumstances but it ended up being an opportunity to develop my skills further and work with a fabulous team. I was given better opportunities to grow and expand my horizons. This most likely would not have happened in my other job.

The final gift that was given to me when I moved on was an opportunity to work with an excellent teaching partner. He has taught me so much about life and work that I will never forget the past five years. All I can say to him is thank you for giving me the strength to grow and change in more positive ways.

Youth give us many gifts. My husband will ask me once in a while if I ever regret not teaching younger children as I had once hoped and dreamed. My answer is always the same. I do not regret one minute of my time teaching high school students. They are young adults just waiting to be encouraged to flourish. I am never going to forget them.

. . .

Points to Remember

- ► Gifts are all around you—you just need to look:
    - – Disabilities can be gifts
    - – Students or clients can give you more back then you give them

- ► Hold onto positive memories to help you through the negative ones:
    - – Gifts can come later after your work with a client is long over
    - – Be patient

- ► Embrace clients with extra energy
    - – They give us more pleasure than we realize
    - – Look at how we can enhance differences

- ► Don't forget to acknowledge co-workers
    - – Compliments can be infectious

- ► Gestures can be powerful when used appropriately:
    - – Use your observation skills—you will see thankfulness all around you

- ► Challenges can be gifts and opportunities
    - – They can present themselves out of adversity

Chapter 10 Challenge & Activity

1. Remembering Positive Encouragement

Gather some mementos that remind you of the positives—good memories, encouragement and support you have been given from the people you work with or from clients over the years. Keep a scrapbook in your office or at home. It is amazing how this will help on challenging days.

Another way to remember the people that touch your heart is through what I would call a binder of encouragement. It is a place to write down stories of the positives or encouragement that staff and clients have given you over the years. I have such a place for most of my students, parents, and colleagues. It was interesting that at the beginning of a school year we had a massive flood that absolutely destroyed my office and practically everything in it. One of the few things that did survive was my binder of encouragement. It is amazing how powerful this encouragement can be. I don't know why it survived but the fact it did makes it all the more special to me.

To take this challenge a step further, send notes of encouragement to some of your colleagues. The positive words may give them strength during a tough day or help them to have a genuinely better outlook. Plus this too can be infectious—it may change the entire group dynamics in a better more positive atmosphere overall and increase morale.

2. Build Your Happy Wall

Start your own happiness wall or bulletin board. Choose artifacts, notes, words, mementos, cards, pictures, etc. that remind you of times when you felt happy. Prepare them in a way that you can refer to them visually especially at times of stress and negativity. It is amazing how much better you will feel when you look back at happy times.

This is an activity you can do with your clients or your own family. It is a great way to get to know the people you work with. Sometimes having other people in the office contribute to such a bulletin board can cheer people up during tough times. The board can also be a reminder to clients to try to remain positive in their lives too.

11

What I Know For Sure

We live in a very busy world where things are changing on a daily basis. Life can be busy, hectic and messy at times. Everyone will go through a personal journey, some with lots of adversity and some with less. My message to you is that you cannot live for only one part of your life. To grow and develop as a human being, you need to make sure you are taking care of all aspects of your life—work, family, friends, yourself. As well, you need to love and cherish all moments because you never know what the future has in store.

Throughout my journey, I have only been able to grow when I paid attention to the gifts and lessons being offered to me. Many times this growth came, unexpectedly, from the not-so-good times.

We are all products of our environments, but it is what we make of ourselves that counts. I remember traveling through Africa and visiting many towns where the people were living in such poverty. We stayed with a family that had a very modest home and they were so proud of it. I was struck by their grace, and how they created a beautiful home out of difficult circumstances. The dignity, strength and resilience they demonstrated were absolutely amazing. It sure put my life in perspective.

As a Helper, you need to pay attention to what is going on around you and make sure you are paying attention to your own needs.

You don't want to fall into the trap of being a workaholic, or burn out. There are support groups to help people deal with these issues as they become more understood. A book written by Diane Fassel, *Working Ourselves to Death*, talks about how we are growing into a community that uses working similar to a drug—we are addicted to the accolades that come with working hard[40] and let's face it, a generation ago it was said that if you work hard you will get ahead in this world. I don't think this is true anymore. People can work hard and still find themselves in difficult circumstances.

Fassel goes on to discuss how we need to learn how to relax, as society seems to be constantly moving faster:

> The inability to relax does not come from work itself, but from incessant work and the way we work. When work is a fix it carries a burden it cannot sustain. Work cannot give us an identity. It cannot *make* us happy. When we expect our work to do things for us that we are not willing to do for ourselves, we become exhausted. More is not better where work is concerned.[41]

This is a growing problem and you just need to be aware of this and make sure you are not falling into this trap. During my work journey, I have noticed time and time again where people are giving all of themselves to their jobs, to the point where there seems to be nothing else in life for them. They work long hours and by the time they get home, they just want to go to bed to sleep to get up and do this all over again the next day. We are a society that has put pressure on people to work harder without giving them tools to do better. This is why everyone wants the quick fix to diet and exercise. We are getting faster and faster. It is time to stop and start taking care of us.

Carl Honoré wrote a book about how to slow down in life.[42] I really believe he is correct. We need to stop moving so fast in life and start working towards a more positive future with less scheduling. If you love schedules then make sure you schedule some time for yourself.

Take the opportunities to go to workshops and learn about yourself.

These can be life-changing. I have been to many that have changed my outlook and fired me up and given me energy for taking my next step in life. Grab onto things in the moment because you never know when the opportunity will present itself again. After participating in the Power Within workshop the message I got loud and clear was to visualize what you want in the future and don't let anything stand in your way to get there. I believe this is a very powerful message and you should continue to strive to be the best you can be without losing yourself along the way.

Remember to value people from all professions and walks of life. You never know what you may learn from people who are around the corner. I went to a business seminar once where people asked what I was going to get out of it, because I was a teacher. My response was there are lessons everywhere; we just need to listen, adapt and learn from people. Many of the lessons I learned about how to work in teams, organization skills, how to inspire others, I was able to integrate into my classroom. Valuable lessons abound; pay attention and you never know what you may learn.

Most of all, be true to yourself. Focus in on your dreams and what gets you up in the morning. There are so many ways we can be Helpers; if you can keep an open mind, then opportunities will follow. It is important to remember dreams will change as you change in life. Don't forget to review your goals and dreams so you are always trying to reach for the moon and live your life to the fullest. Dreams and goals change as you grow and develop so make sure you review them. Don't let your life become stagnant.

The adversity we face is what growth is based on. I have often talked to people who have shared tough stories with me about how they wish they could go back to the past and change things because life would have been so much simpler now. The reality is that your life may not have changed for the better had you not gone through the tough stuff. You need to leave the past in the past—yes, you need to deal with the feelings and emotions, but then you need to let the past go. You cannot change your past, so it is important to focus on your present and the future.

Many people have talked about the power of forgiveness. I believe this is an important part of our journey. One time I was holding on to a grudge where someone had been very belittling to me, and it was eating me alive. I focused on that every time we were out with a group and it made me angry, but once I was able to let go of the anger, I felt like a new person. I changed the way I viewed people and had a better understanding of the power of forgiveness. This can really change your life from a place of negativity to a place of feeling positive. So the next time you catch yourself being angry at someone for a long time and holding a grudge—let it go. You will be amazed at how much this decision can and will change your life and make you feel a lot better.

When you are able to take responsibility for your actions then you are helping yourself. Remember you just need to try to learn from your mistakes and actions and not dwell on the negative aspects of what has happened. Staying focused on the positives in life can only enhance the situations you are in and your life in general. Don't get bogged down with the small stuff as there is enough big stuff that can grab your attention.

I cannot believe my dreams and goals have changed but that is the way life is—you need to make changes to keep up with the reality of life. Sometimes paths are chosen for you or they drop into your lap and at other times you have to create new opportunities for yourself. So be prepared to take on the new and exciting activities that may come your way. Grab opportunities when they present themselves because you may not get another chance to do so.

Most importantly, don't sit on the sidelines of your life. You need to go out there and do things that make you excited. As a Helper you are given lessons daily on how fast a life could change for people. Sadly, there are a lot more people out there struggling than we would like to admit, but don't dismiss them. They can teach you many things about themselves and you. Just remember not to ride their roller coaster. Life will pass you by quickly unless you stop and smell the roses or take the opportunities that are given to you. If none are presented then you need to make your opportunities happen. You can usually find a way to create them!

So what I know for sure from my life is to stay focused on the prize, and always continue to give out praise and positive encouragement. Continue to strive for what you believe in. If you believe what you are doing is right then it most likely is the right thing to do. Follow your instincts, because they are generally correct. Passion for your work will drive you to do better in both your life and career. If you believe in what you are doing then the stressful times are well worth it when they are occurring.

Laughing and smiling daily is a must. If you can look at yourself at the end of the day and be happy with who you are and what you have accomplished that day then it makes this work all worthwhile. With more pleasure and enjoyment, your health will be better and you will be better able to handle the stress in your life. You will also be more positive about yourself and your life.

Making sure you have some sort of balance is important. When life is out of balance then you need to be sure to bring it back into balance. Sometimes this may be easier said than done. Try to develop checks and balances where you can reassess your life, goals and dreams. This way, when your life is out of balance, you can catch yourself before it goes on too long and you risk losing your values.

My journey has brought me to many new beginnings, one of which is this book. New beginnings can bring about new growth and wonderful experiences. Everyone will have their own journey and it is important to take the time to relax and enjoy this journey you are on; live your life to the fullest. Value the work you do and most of all value you as a person. Finally, remember to help others, without losing yourself.

. . .

Appendix A: Anger Questions Log

Think about three times when you were angry. Ask yourself the following questions:

1. Is this worth my attention?
2. Am I justified being angry about the situation?
3. Do I have an effective response?

Record the information below.

Situation #1 _____

_____

_____

_____

1. Attention? _____ 2. Justified? _____ 3. Effective Response _____

Situation #2 _____

_____

_____

_____

1. Attention? _____ 2. Justified? _____ 3. Effective Response _____

Situation #3 _____

_____

_____

_____

1. Attention? _____ 2. Justified? _____ 3. Effective Response _____

REMEMBER: If you answer no to any of these questions, then it is not appropriate to be angry.

Appendix B: Suggestions for Accessing Professional Counselling

Here are some suggestions when seeking professional support services. I would start with those resources recommended to you through work. There are also helpful websites like the College of Psychologists, as well as forums and review sites that discuss counselling. Finding a good counsellor is a personal decision and can be difficult at times. The website www.athealth.com suggests counselling when you:

- Spend 5 out of 7 days feeling unhappy
- Regularly cannot sleep at night
- Are taking care of a parent or a child and the idea crosses your mind that you may want to hit that person
- Place an elder in a nursing home or in alternative care
- Have lost someone or something (such as a job)
- Have a chronic or acute medical illness
- Can no longer prioritize what is most important in your life
- Feel that you can no longer manage your stress

Some things you should look for in counselling:

- What do I want to get out of my sessions? Be upfront about that from the beginning.
- Do I want group or individual sessions?
- Is my counsellor communicating well so that I understand what is going on?
- Are the sessions focused on my issues?
- Am I willing to move forward with the counsellor's suggestions?
- Have I been clear about what my goals are and what I want help with in the first place?

Many counsellors believe these are working sessions, with each person doing their fair share of the work. It is suggested you start with individual counselling and in consultation with the counsellor decide if group or individual would be your best options. Whatever type of session you want, make sure you feel comfortable with the counsellor you have chosen.

For more information about counsellors in your area, contact your family physician or go on your local website for registered counsellors. If you have been victimized, you can contact your local victim services to help find someone that has experience in this type of counselling.

Appendix C: Personal Networking

Professional
_____
_____
_____
_____
_____
_____
_____

Community
People
_____
_____
_____
_____
_____
_____

You

Family
_____
_____
_____
_____
_____
_____
_____
_____

Friends
_____
_____
_____
_____
_____
_____
_____
_____

Appendix D: Decision Making

From the past week, write down ten decisions you made.

1. _____

2. _____

3. _____

4. _____

5. _____

6. _____

7. _____

8. _____

9. _____

10. _____

Using the chart below, write each decision into the appropriate column.

Positive Decisions	Negative Decisions

Appendix E: Resources on Dealing with Relationships

There are a number of community service organizations that deal with relationship counselling. It would be appropriate for you to look up your local services online. One place to start would be to talk to other couples who may have gone through similar circumstances, contact a local counselling centre with suggestions or ask your family doctor. Here are some resources I would recommend for this topic:

1. *Relationship Rescue; A Seven-Step Strategy for Reconnecting with Your Partner,* by Dr. Philip McGraw

    There is also a workbook that can be used alongside the book. This book discusses how to get back the spark you may have once had and how to strengthen your relationship by working on yourself first. Once you have gotten your own power back, you have to both be willing to participate in the program. Dr. Phil wants people to get real with each other and be present in the relationship. It is a great read and step towards building and taking your relationship to the next level.

2. *The Seven Principles for Making Marriage Work; A Practical Guide from the Country's Foremost Relationship Expert,* by John Gottman and Nan Silver

    This book is descriptive of Gottman's experience observing married couples over many years. He has scientifically looked at how relationships work and broken down how they are successful. He presents his findings in the book. It also has quizzes and exercises to help you work through your relationship.

3. *Men are From Mars, Women are From Venus; The Classic Guide to Understanding the Opposite Sex,* by John Gray

This is a classic that has been around for some years. John Gray discusses how couples are successful when they accept they are from the opposite sex and respect each other's differences. He is a counsellor who has been working with couples throughout his career. Gray focuses on how to develop good communication skills and styles worth looking at if you want to strengthen your relationship with your spouse or significant other.

4. *Don't Sweat the Small Stuff in Love; Simple Ways to Nurture and Strengthen Your Relationships While Avoiding the Habits That Break Down Your Loving Connection,* by Richard Carlson and Kristine Carlson

This book focuses on using humour to avoid the popular pitfalls that happen in a relationship. The authors discuss how not to pick apart your partner but appreciate them and become a good listener. The Carlsons also suggest that by looking out for each other, you can help your partner move to the next level in your relationship. It is worth a read as it helps to show the importance of a relationship and how the little things are not worth your attention.

There are many more resources out there for you to look through. When choosing one, be prepared to put in the time just as if you have gone to a therapy session. Remember that it will be worth every moment if you are able to fix the relationship. There will be groups and supports within your own community. Don't hesitate to look for them.

Appendix F: Understanding What is Important to You

Decide ten things or people you value the most and list them.

1. _____

2. _____

3. _____

4. _____

5. _____

6. _____

7. _____

8. _____

9. _____

10. _____

Make sure they are in order of importance. Now delete five items; what remains are your true top five items.

Below is a table for the group activity Think, Pair, Share. Start by ranking the items in column A. Then with a partner rank the items from 1–10 between the two of you in column B. You must agree. Finally in small groups rank the items from 1–10 in column C and again you must all agree. You can change the items you choose for the activity to be more appropriate for the group if needed.

You have been stranded on a desert island. You can assume there is limitless water and bland food that provides all your nutritional needs. How would you rank the following items?

Items	A	B	C
Your favourite food			
Your favourite drink			
Family members (up to 2)			
Friends (up to 2)			
Hygiene items			
Blankets and pillows			
Endless supply of books			
Endless supply of movies			
Endless supply of video games			
Computer with only an Internet browser			

Don't forget to debrief when the activity is complete. This should spark some interesting dialogue.

Appendix G: *Me, Myself and I* Syndrome

This describes every teenager at one point when they are growing up. Their life becomes all about themselves and they seem to have tunnel vision. They are not aware of how their actions are taking away from your life and how they may be causing you stress because at this point it is all about them.

After working with teenagers for many years, I have come up with some solutions to this syndrome that may help get the family through the *Me, Myself and I* years. They are as follows:

1. Have a candid conversation about this topic long before it becomes an issue. Create a hand signal or gesture to use with your child when either the parent or the teen is acting in a way that is ignoring the needs of the other person. For example, when the teen is acting in a very selfish manner, the parent could tap their head or give them a wave or snap their fingers. When the teen feels the parent is acting in a selfish manner, the teen could rub their nose or clap their hands. The agreement has to be made that each individual will stop what they are doing or saying in the moment and think about why the opposite person thinks that what they are doing is selfish. Be sure to talk about this at a later time to discuss how each other can compromise so everyone's needs are met.

2. Develop a contract between the parents (or Helper) and the teen. Think of consequences ahead of time in case the contract is broken by someone not living up to their obligations. For example, if the youth wants a ride to work, then they need to make sure dinner is made and the dishes are washed so the

adult will drive them to work. If they do not do these chores ahead of time, then the adult has the right to refuse to drive them.

3. Have a humourous conversation about what the youth sounds like when they are making unrealistic demands. For example, exaggerate what they say and do when they are asking for things that do not fit into your schedule as the adult. Thus when you are sitting down for dinner the next time, imitate how they sound or what they say. After everyone has a good laugh and the youth may or may not be acting defensive about how they sound, lay out what you need from each other to make sure things at home run smoother and everyone's needs are being met. This may help smooth the way for less rocky times if everyone is involved with the decision making.

Appendix H: Boundaries Assignment Template

Think of twenty activities you have done in the past month. Write each activity in the appropriate column based on whether or not the activities are in your best interest.

Activities That Were in my Best Interest	Activities That Were NOT in my Best Interest

Put a "**P**" beside any activity that was breaking a Personal Boundary.

Put a "**W**" beside any activity that was breaking a Work or Professional Boundary.

Now think of some areas where you might be able to improve your personal boundaries with friends and colleagues. Practice and then take this information forward so the next time someone tries to break the boundaries you are prepared for them.

Note: There are other boundary categories but when starting out, it is easier to separate the boundaries into two categories. If you want to go further into boundary work, you may want to classify them into even more specific areas such as categories of boundaries at work—public work boundaries, co-worker boundaries, or management boundaries.

Appendix I: Resources on Developing Skills

There are many resources on skill-building. Some good ones that I came across doing the research for this book were:

Exploring Feelings; Cognitive Behaviour Therapy to Manage ANGER, by Tony Attwood

Feeling Good; The New Mood Therapy, by David Burns

The Behaviour Disorder IEP Companion; Objectives, Interventions, and Strategies, by Molly Lyle Brown

Impulse Control; Stop and Think, by Tonia Caselman

The Seven Habits of Highly Effective Teens, by Sean Covey

Life Strategies for Teens, by Jay McGraw

Fighting Invisible Tigers; A Stress Management Guide for Teens, by Earl Hipp (there is a workbook that goes with this book)

Taming Worry Dragons; A Manual for Children, Parents, and Other Coaches, by Jane Garland and Sandra Clark

Appendix J: Improving Our Decision Skills When Making Mistakes

The next time you make a mistake, answer the following questions:

1. What was the mistake?

2. What were the specific details?

3. Were you happy with the outcome? Why or why not?

4. What could you do to improve your response next time?

5. What happened prior to you making the mistake? Was anything else bothering you that could have triggered your reactions?

6. Have you made this mistake before? Was your response the same the last time you made this mistake?

7. Things you want to look out for next time you are put in a similar situation.

Appendix K: Self-Talk, Self-Visualization & Meditation

Here is an outline of how to practice each of these methods. There are many more examples that you can get out of books or off the Internet. Just remember that a method may not work for you, but if you can find one that will help you with relaxing and focusing better, use that method the next time things feel very stressful for you.

Self-Talk

Self-talk is a tricky activity because it is really just you rehearsing for a situation that makes you feel anxious. This is a time when you want to talk yourself out of the negativity. Another area most people don't do well with is positive self-talk. I give an example of each category and hopefully this will help you to start using more positive self-talk in many aspects of your life.

Scenario #1

You are scared of heights and a group wants to go hiking on the side of a mountain. You love hiking and really want to be part of the excursion, so you start saying positive things about the trip such as,

- I can do this
- I will not get hurt
- I am going to enjoy the amazing view
- We are taking every precaution so if something goes wrong I can do this
- When I am feeling anxious, I will do some deep breathing to help try to relax my body so that it does not seem so difficult

Using these techniques and statements before you go on the trip can help keep you focused on why you wanted to go on the trip in the first place. Also, using self-visualization of all the positive aspects of the outing can help with keeping yourself calm while on the hike.

Scenario #2

When people make negative comments about you, are you the type of person who believes what the other person is saying? If you are, it is time to stop. If you need some positive comments to start you off, here is one that you can try—My smile is beautiful. I am going to smile every day and look at myself in the mirror and state, "I have a beautiful smile and I look gorgeous when I smile." Be sure you make your positive statement right when you wake up each morning to ensure it is the first thing you think of when you wake up and make sure it is the last thing you hear before you go to bed. When you have truly believed this statement and it is ingrained in you, begin to start loving another feature of your body such as your eyes. Tell yourself, "I have beautiful eyes that show how wonderful I am on the inside to the entire world," every morning and every evening. Continue this until you completely believe it.

Something to remember about positive self-talk is that it takes fourteen days to create a habit and fourteen weeks to break one, thus it only takes two weeks to make the positive words a habit. This is by following the instructions daily and not missing a day. You will be amazed how much better you feel after creating these positive habits.

Self-Visualization

Self-Visualization is usually used to help focus on things you want to accomplish and how to attain them. This is a great activity to do after a meditation session when your mind is clear. You don't have to do them in that order but I have found it is much easier to focus when you have a clear mind and are feeling relaxed.

Take a deep breath in and slowly release it at least ten times. Continue to make sure you have cleared your mind of any and all thoughts that may stop you from focusing on the task at hand. Keep breathing and letting go of your thoughts so you are only focusing on your chest going up and down.

Now imagine you are doing something you have always wanted to do and the feelings that it brings you. Make those feelings fill your body with happiness and joy. Now see yourself doing this activity in your head. Think of all your senses and how you can feel better about yourself by doing this activity. Where will this journey take you, what are you going to accomplish doing this activity? Answer all those questions and feel the joy of the activity.

When you have seen every aspect and used all your senses to imagine what they would feel like when you are doing this activity, write down or draw yourself doing the activity. Remember to write down the senses you felt and how you were using them to enjoy the moments more.

Finally, think of how you will be able to make this a reality. What do you have to do to make this work? For example, if you have always wanted to go to Paris and you have imagined yourself standing in front of the Eiffel Tower, then what are the steps that you need to make or take to attain this vision? Make a list and keep working on this dream until it becomes a reality.

Meditation

You can try this activity individually or with a partner. It is usually easier to envision with your eyes closed but that is a personal choice. Finding a space with no distractions is a key factor in aiding you with your ability to focus. This is just one example of an exercise. There are many out there that you can try but this one seems to work the best for me. Relax and enjoy!

Sit in a quiet room with little to no distractions. Dim the lights or use just natural light—whichever helps you concentrate. Then start taking in deep breaths. When breathing, focus on your lungs expanding and your breath coming out of your body. Lose yourself in your breathing. Count to ten slowly while focusing on your breath coming in and out of your body. Imagine all of the stressors from your day leaving your body every time you exhale.

Continue breathing after counting to ten. Imagine a white light or a flame of fire. This light or fire can be seen starting at your toes. Let it circle each of the five toes and feel all the toxins of your body leaving. You can feel the tension and the muscles in your toes start to relax. Now this light or flame is going to move to the balls of your feet. You can feel the muscle tension relax and the muscles are starting to let go. Every tension, every struggle, every stressor, is leaving the body through your toes. Keep breathing and focus on the entire foot letting go of anything that is bothering you. Deep breath in and relax.

Now this light or flame is on the balls of your feet. It is circling them, running through them. All the tension in your feet is gone—you can feel it melting away and your body relaxing. Your feet are on the floor totally relaxed and you have let all of the worries go and are just breathing. Now the light/flame is moving to your ankles. It is circling the ankles taking all of the muscle tension out and helping you to relax. You can feel all your muscles tensing and then relaxing; the muscles in your feet now feel like they are attached to the floor. They are not heavy, just relaxed.

Continue breathing in and out. Now imagine this light/flame moving up the lower leg to your calf. It is circling around working on repairing all of the muscles you used today and you are totally relaxed. All the pain you have felt today is leaving your body through your feet and you are feeling overwhelmingly relaxed. This light/flame is taking over the lower leg and helping it to release and relax. Keep taking deep breaths in and out.

Now the light/flame is circling around the knee. Letting the tension in the knee seize up and relax. Taking away any pain or aching you might feel there. You are taking all the pain or tension and having it leave the body through the feet that are relaxed and not heavy. Finally when you are ready the light/flame is moving up the legs to the thigh. Circling those large muscles in the legs and helping the body to let go of the pain and strain of your day through you entire leg, letting you relax. Keep taking deep breaths in and out. This light/flame is circling and helping your entire leg relax and let go.

Continue breathing in and out. Now the light is going through your torso and buttocks area. Let go of the tension and muscle strain that may be felt. You can feel the tightness start to lessen and all of the pain and tension is leaving your body. Now your whole lower body should feel relaxed and you are focusing on the pain leaving and your breathing getting deeper. Continue the breathing—deep breath in and slowly release the breath out.

After two very deep breaths, start to focus on your abdomen. See the light/flame circling and making your lower stomach feel like all the pain or muscle aches are going away. They are leaving the body. You are not worried about anything but relieving the tension in your muscles. Deep breath in and slowly release out. Now think of your lower back. All the tension and muscle strain you may have caused it. Think of the light/flame circling around your problem areas and letting all of the tension out of the body. Deep breath in and slowly release. You should not feel anything below the waist but relaxed muscles. Keep breathing.

Think of the light/flame moving up the back and all down your spine. Like someone is taking warm water down each of your vertebras and forcing you to relax. All the pain and tension in your back is going away from your body and in its place is a calm and relaxed body. All your stress and tension from life is slowly leaving the body and not going to return for a long time. All of the muscles in your back are relaxing. The light/flame is moving up and down your spine taking all of your worries away.

Now the light/flame is moving to your chest and the front of your body is relaxing so everything below your shoulders should feel like it is floating and there are no cares in the world when it comes to your body. Continue to take deep breaths in and slowly release them. This light/flame is taking all the toxins from your body and you are slowly breathing them out of it. Every muscle should be feeling very relaxed and there is not a care in the world right not but you and your breathing.

The light/flame is now moving into the shoulders, circling all of the muscles and releasing all of the tension you may be feeling. All of the stress and burdens you have are leaving your body and the muscles are starting to let go. Feel yourself continuing to relax and your breathing getting deeper and deeper. Now the light/flame is starting to move down the arms circling the upper arm. All the tension is leaving through the arms and out into the atmosphere. Deep breath in and slowly release it. Feel the light/flame move down to your wrist and feel all of the muscle strain of the day and let it go. Breathe all the toxins out of your body. Now the light/flame is circling your hands and relaxing them to the point that you are not able to feel them anymore. All of the muscles in the hand are starting to relax and release any and all toxins. The light/flame is moving down each finger individually. You should feel the release of anything you have been holding on to let go through the fingers and into the air. Your tension or toxins are gone out of your body. Deep breath in and slowly release.

After having the light/flame travel down each finger, the light/flame will continue to move back up the arm and into the neck. You want to continue to release all the tension you may feel in your neck. Any tense muscles should be letting go and releasing all the tension and stress you may have been holding in that area. Let it go. Deep breath in and slowly release. Continue to circle all of the neck muscles. If there is extra tension and stress let it go. Continue with the deep breathing and let everything go that you may be feeling.

Now have the light/flame move and circle your entire head. Have any tensions or stressors leave your mind and feel your head start to relax. Deep breath in and slowly release. Continue to get rid of any toxic thoughts or feelings you have had in your head and let everything go out into the atmosphere and disappear. Continue to breathe and focus on this. Now imagine an egg is cracking and running all over your face to help the light/flame relax all the tensions you may feel there. Deep breath in and slowly release. Spend another minute to continue to relax your face.

The light/flame is now going to move into the mouth and to your throat. Relax all the muscles there so you can just focus on breathing in and out. After circling the throat, the light/flame is moving down your wind pipe into the lungs with you continuing to breathe in and out. Focus on seeing the breath take all your stressors, toxins, and pain from the body and letting it go in the atmosphere. Deep breath in and slowly release. Continue to watch all your worries and toxic thoughts leave through this breath and to not return. Deep breath in and slowly release.

When you are ready and feel it is time, you can open your eyes and take some more deep breaths in and slowly release them. Say something positive to yourself and enjoy the rest of your day. You have earned it and deserve only the best from this moment on!

Appendix L: Is Counselling Working for you?

1. On a scale of 1–10, 1 being not well at all and 10 being working extremely well, how would you rate the counselling sessions and why?

2. What are some of the things that are working for you in your sessions?

3. What are some of the things that are not working for you in your sessions?

4. What are some of the areas that you personally would like to improve on?

5. Do you want to go back for more sessions or would you like to be referred to someone else?

6. What are some suggestions you could make to the counsellor to improve your sessions?

Appendix M: Humour Resources

There are many resources that can help with your sense of humour. Here are some of my favourites that I came across during my research:

Get Weird! 101 Innovative Ways to Make Your Company a Great Place to Work, by John Putzier

> This resource discusses ways to create a culture of fun and innovation. There are great ideas that help to develop ways to incorporate humour and enjoy getting up each day to go to work.

Snap Out of It! 101 Ways to Get Out of Your Rut & Into Your Groove, by Ilene Segalove

> The activities can be used to help you out of a low mood to change your outlook to a more positive one. It is definitely worth a look if you are having difficulties figuring out ways to pull yourself out of the mundane.

Relax—You May Only Have a Few Minutes Left; Using the Power of Humor to Overcome Stress in Your Life and Work, by Loretta LaRoche

> This book helps show how humour can overcome stress. She also has a video performance that talks about overcoming stress called *The Joy of Stress*, which is worth a look to help reduce stress in the workplace. She makes some great suggestions in both resources.

The Joy Diet; 10 Daily Practices for a Happier Life, by Martha Beck

The 10 practices are practical and some do not take too much effort to implement; the results may surprise you.

The Laughing Classroom; Everyone's Guide To Teaching With Humor and Play, by Diane Loomans and Karen Kolberg

This book discusses ways to help make your classroom a more humourous place to work. It has many activities you could do with your students or in small groups of young people. Some of the activities can be adapted for groups of adults.

I Love Your Laugh; Finding the Light in My Screwball Life, by Jessica Holmes

This book is a memoir of the things she found humourous in her everyday life. It is very entertaining.

Appendix N: The Goal Setting Ladder

End Goal:

_____

_____

_____

_____

_____

Where You are Starting From:

_____

Notes

1. Anne Wilson Schaef and Diane Fassel. *The Addictive Organization; Why We Overwork, Cover Up, Pick Up the Pieces, Please the Boss & Perpetuate Sick Organizations.* (New York: Harper Collins, 1988), 74.

2. Schaef and Fassel: 74 & 75.

3. The Power Within is a series of events featuring motivational speakers who present around the world on topics to help release your inner self and developing a more positive focus in life. For more information go to their website: www.powerwithin.com.

4. Pamela E. Butler. *Self-Assertion for Women; The classic Guide that has Helped Thousands of Women Take Charge of Their Lives Revised Edition.* (San Francisco: Harper Collins, 1992), 8.
   *** All information written in this chapter, referring to Pamela Butler, comes from this book.

5. Butler: 119.

6. Philip C. McGraw. *Life Strategies; Doing What Works, Doing What Matters.* New York: Hyperion, 1999.
   *** For further information about the Ten Life Laws, you can access the book or his website: www.drphil.com.

7. McGraw: 192.

8. "Anger" 20/20. *So Angry You Could Die.* Journal Graphics, 1993.
   *** This video is part of the Anger Management Program the Unloading Zone. It is through this training that I have gained access to this information.

9. John M. Grohol. http://psychcentral.com/blog/archives/2008/08/11/asking-for-help.

10. Joel Zeff. *Make the Right Choice; Creating a Positive, Innovative, and Productive Work Life.* (Hoboken, New Jersey: John Wiley & Sons, Inc., 2007), 96.

11. Appreciative Inquiry is a form of evaluation where you look at the positive things a company may be doing and build upon that to make a company do better. One of the founders and a good resource on the topic is Cooperrider and Stavros, who wrote, *Appreciative Inquiry Handbook.* There is also a Centre for Appreciative Inquiry. For more information: www.centerforappreciativeinquiry.net.

12. Julie Morgenstern. *Time Management from the Inside Out; The Foolproof System for Taking Control of Your Schedule—And Your Life. Second Edition.* (New York: Henry Holt and Company, 2004), 13. *** The other book Julie Morgenstern wrote was *Organization from the Inside Out.* Also a good resource for people trying to move ahead and streamline their time.

13. Elaine St. James. *Simplify Your Work Life; Ways to Change the Way You Work So You Have More Time to Live.* (New York: Hyperion, 2001), xiv–xv.

14. Dr. Bernie S. Siegel. *101 Exercises for the Soul; A Divine Workout Plan for Body, Mind, and Spirit.* (Novato, California: New World Library, 2005), 178.

15. Sam Horn. *What's Holding you Back? Thirty Days to Having the Courage and Confidence to Do What You Want, Meet Whom You Want, and Go Where You Want.* New York: St. Martin's Griffin, 1997. *** She has also written a lot of books on how to prevent conflict that all have very unique titles; *Tongue Fu* and *Take the Bully by the Horns,* to name a few. Both are pretty good reads and will help you with your everyday life. Sam Horn is a speaker on an international scale and you can contact her about upcoming workshops she is giving at samhorn.com.

16. Jan Black and Greg Enns. *Better Boundaries; Owning and Treasuring Your Life.* (Oakland: New Harbingers Publications Inc., 1997), 9.

17. Black and Enns: 63.

18. Harriet B. Braiker. *The Disease to Please; Curing the People-Pleasing Syndrome.* New York: McGraw-Hill, 2001.
*** If you think you suffer from a disease to please, this is a good reference for you to use to come up with strategies on how to stop helping everyone but yourself.

19. Anthony Robbins is a world renowned author and speaker. He presents many workshops on developing your own power. If you would like to know more information about him or when he may be in your area, go to www.anthonyrobbins.com

20. David D. Burns. *Ten Days to Self-Esteem.* New York: Harper Collins, 1999.

21. Joan Borysenko. *Guilt is the Teacher, Love is the Lesson.* (New York: Time Warner Company, 1990), 9.

22. Borysenko: 9–10.

23. L. M. Montgomery. *Anne of Green Gables.* (Toronto: Bantam Classic Edition, 1987), 176.

24. *Alcoholics Anonymous Fourth Edition.* New York: Alcoholics Anonymous World Services , Inc., 2001.
*** A good read for those who feel they may be suffering from addictions. This is what the Alcoholics Anonymous community has dubbed the Big Book. This book outlines the twelve steps of recovery in detail and discusses how people can access support and assistance with each step.

25. Ross W.Greene. *The Explosive Child; A New Approach for Understanding and Parenting Easily Frustrated, Chronically Inflexible Children—Revised and Updated.* New York: Harper Collins, 2010.

26. Susan Jeffers. *Feel the Fear... and Do It Anyway. 20th Anniversary Edition.* (New York: Ballantine Books, 2007), 62.

27. Jeffers: 65.

28. Susan Jeffers. *Life is Huge; Laughing, Loving and Learning from it All.* (Santa Monica: Jeffers Press, 2004), 81.

29. Jeffers: 86.

30. Polly Shulman. "Crack Me Up! Breaking the Humor Code." *Psychology Today.* August 2006: 73.

31. Shulman: 69.

32. The Power of Women is similar to the Power Within. They have positive female speakers come and discuss issues that face women in the world. For information about when they will be in your area just do an Internet search "Power of Women" or contact your local women's groups.

33. www.jessicaholmes.com

34. www.lorettalaroche.com

35. Cheryl Richardson. *Take Time for Your Life; A 7-Step Program for Creating the Life You Want.* (New York: Broadway Books, 1999: 54. *** All information from this paragraph comes from this book.

36. To develop this challenge further, you could do the activities in Cheryl Richardson's book discussed in Chapter 2 Setting your Priorities. In this chapter she goes step-by-step as to how you can understand where your time goes and whether or not this is currently working for you. These are well worth a look if you feel time is escaping you.

37. Parkinson's disease is a neurological disease that affects the nerve cells in the brain. It can be debilitating as the patients will have difficulties with body movements. For more information on this disease go to www.parkinsonsdisease.org

38. Michael J. Fox. *Always Looking Up; The Adventures of an Incurable Optimist*. (New York: Hyperion, 2009), 6.
***Fox also wrote a second biography of the first part of his life called *Lucky Man*. Both are worth the read as he shows how life can give you many gifts even when issues are very difficult to deal with.

39. www.muscle.ca/national/muscular-dystrophy.

40. Diane Fassel. *Working Ourselves to Death; the High Cost of Workaholism & the Rewards of Recovery*. San Francisco: Harper Collins, 1990.

41. Fassel: 35.

42. Carl Honoré. *In the Praise of Slow; How a Worldwide Movement is Challenging the Cult of Speed*. Toronto: Vintage Canada, 2004.
*** This book has a lot of suggestions of how we can slow down and start living more of our life and enjoy it.

About the Author

Debbie Holmes is an educator, speaker, and author of *How to Help Others without Losing Yourself.* For the past 16 years, Debbie has taught academics and life skills to youth and adults in the Surrey School District, one of the largest school districts in western Canada.

With an extensive history of working with youth in the area of career development, Debbie consults with school districts to improve district resources and programs. Debbie regularly hosts workshops on strengthening community programs for youth at risk, and she is a frequent presenter at the Career Education Society Conference.

Debbie is also an educator of community-based helpers, teaching strategies to prevent and reduce helper burnout. As a member of the Train-the-Trainer Series team, Debbie worked directly with helper-educators to assist them with the skill development of their front line workers.

A member of the Crime Reduction Strategy Committee for the developmentally disabled in the City of Surrey, Debbie is currently developing an education plan and a court case managerial position for the B.C. Provincial Criminal Justice System.

CPSIA information can be obtained
at www.ICGtesting.com
Printed in the USA
LVOW04s1821240616

493965LV00002B/6/P